idea
Library Learning Information

To renew this item call:
0115 929 3388
or visit
www.ideastore.co.uk

TOWER HAMLETS

Created and managed by Tower Hamlets Council

My Kind of Food

My Kind of Food

Recipes I Love to Cook at Home

John Torode

headline

Dedicated to my children –
Marcel, Casper, Jonah and Loulou

Contents

This book is about how I cook at home, and the chapters reflect me and the things in life I love – it's how I eat.

Introduction

This book, *My Kind Of Food*, is a document of my life in food, and of my travels and my loves.

Why did I decide to write it? Because cooking is what I do and what I have always done. I do it professionally and it is my way of life, but cooking is also the way I relax. It is the thing I dream about the most; it makes me smile and it is something that I am proud to be able to do well. Yes, I am a judge on MasterChef, where I taste thousands of dishes, and yes, I am a trained chef, which has had me commanding some of the biggest brigades a kitchen has ever seen. Yes, I have travelled the world and cooked on TV and at food shows up and down the country, but in my heart I am a home cook. I do most of my cooking at home – for my friends and family and for me, so this is a collection of those recipes. It is the food I love, that I cook all the time, and it is a book full of recipes that have a story, a soul and a reason.

I also wanted you to know me and what my kind of food actually is. It's not a single style – French, Asian, Australasian or British – it's not modern, old-fashioned or classic; it's a mix of all these things. And at its core is a boy who loved to cook with his Nanna.

The food I had as a child was not complicated but by heck it was tasty. I have been very lucky to have eaten in some of the most amazing places and restaurants in the world, but the food I ate as a boy – my Nanna's home cooking – stands firmly in my heart as some of the best I have ever tasted. I still make the roast chicken that I learned to cook with her and it sits proudly in these pages, along with many other childhood favourites, such as my dad's lamb fritters. And as I have grown up I have also discovered new worlds of flavour, of spice, opulence and indulgence, and those recipes are here too.

I want the book to reflect the way we live today, not some fairytale kitchen with helpers and washer-uppers and gizmos and gadgets. These recipes are for everyday kitchens like yours and mine. You won't need lots of equipment: a few pots and pans, a large casserole (I love my Le Creuset!), a sharp knife and a big substantial wooden chopping board will see you through most of the recipes.

The chapters, too, mirror how I cook. Sometimes I wear shorts; some days I wear wellies (sometimes together!) Often I have to wear a suit and sometimes I don't; my food is simply me – variable. First and foremost, I absolutely love breakfast. I love it at any time of the day but on a weekend, when I get a chance to sleep in, my Aussie roots come to the fore and I cook brunch. It's more than a meal to me, it reminds me of Australia, so I have dedicated a whole chapter to my favourite breakfast and brunch recipes.

Everything in this book has been cooked many, many times over – in my own kitchen, for my family and friends. I have done all the hard work and played with the dishes to make them as easy as possible. There is a big chapter on meals for the family that absolutely sums this up. It's full of feasts for hungry crowds and pots of deliciousness that will make enough so that some can be frozen and pulled out in case of a culinary emergency. And we all have those! My children are a great barometer of what is good so all their favourites are in here too.

There's also a chapter for when you haven't got much time. It's for when the shopping has been done and you're at home but with very little time to get a meal together. As a parent, I know that having to do baths, read books and help with homework as well as get food on the table can be stressful, so I hope this chapter will take a bit of the pressure off, or just help those of you that get home late and need dinner fast and without fuss.

Sometimes I have time, sometimes I am in a rush, and sometimes I forget things – doing the shopping, for example. Like all people I am busy and at times I get home and haven't had a chance to get to the shops, but the kids still need feeding, so there is a chapter that makes use of what's likely to be found lurking in my fridge/store cupboard/freezer. I don't need food to be posh every day, it just needs to be tasty. And because where I'm from we also spend loads of time eating outdoors, there's a whole chapter of recipes you can cook on the barbie, or that are designed for eating when the sun shines (with contingency plans for how to cook the dishes indoors too – I've lived in the UK long enough to know from experience that we can't rely on the British weather).

For the adventurer and the conquering cook, I have also included 'Leave Overnight', a short chapter dedicated to those who have the time and are happy to do some prep work in order to cook up a storm.

Finally, of course, there is a puds section too, and these range from a basic custard, a steamed pudding and popcorn, to upside-down cakes and jam doughnuts, which are one of my favourite things in the world, and to die for.

As a chef I have never wanted stars or hats or rosettes, all I have wanted is for the people I cook for to smile and say 'That's delicious'; 'Is there any more?'; 'Thanks

Cook's notes

All butter is salted unless otherwise stated.

All eggs are medium unless otherwise stated.

All milk is full-fat unless otherwise stated.

All sugar is granulated unless otherwise stated.

Tomato sauce means ketchup (it's an Aussie thing)!

Thick yoghurt means you can choose the type you like – I like mine full-fat and rich.

Where a recipe calls for dark chocolate, I've only specified the percentage of cocoa solids if the recipe really needs a particularly high percentage. Chocolate can be pricey so I'll leave the choices up to you.

All oven temperatures are for a conventional oven. If you are using a fan oven, reduce the temperature by 20°C.

Papa'; or 'Can you show me how to make it?' And that's where this book comes in. I want you to feel at ease about cooking everything, almost as if I were there showing you how to do it. Though please use my recipes as you will. If you're a seasoned cook, you don't have to follow them exactly, perhaps just use them for inspiration, but for the beginner I hope that I can hold your hand and help you cook with confidence.

Cooking should not be a chore and it certainly shouldn't be daunting. It's a time for you to let go, and get lost in the sights and smells that nature has gifted us.

So my parting word is get that pot in the oven, pour yourself a glass of wine and enjoy the smells that will flood your kitchen as you chat through your day with those you love. Cooking is a joy and I really hope you find yours in my book.

The Aussie in me is all about eating through the morning. My perfect day starts slowly – if breakfast is the meal of kings, then brunch is the food of emperors.

brunch
to lunch

The Bloody Mary (it's a meal in itself)

A Bloody Mary works because it gets the heart beating. It must be well seasoned and really cold, so you need plenty of ice, and the little bit of vodka floating on top makes it extra special. This is quite a spicy one; but you can spice it up even more if you like. Not for the faint-hearted. (There's a double shot of vodka per person!)

Makes 2 beauties*

lots of ice

120ml vodka, plus a little extra to float

1 teaspoon grated fresh horseradish or 1 teaspoon grated horseradish from a jar

2 big shakes of celery salt

juice of ½ lemon

600ml tomato juice

1 tablespoon Worcestershire sauce

10 drops of Tabasco sauce

loads of black pepper

celery sticks, to serve (optional)

* brunch always starts with a Bloody Mary

Put loads of ice into a jug, then add the vodka, horseradish, celery salt and lemon juice. Now add the tomato juice then the Worcestershire sauce, Tabasco and pepper – in that order. Stir well.

Fill two tall glasses with ice and pour over the Bloody Mary. Float a little extra vodka on top if you're really cheeky.

Classically served with a stick of celery.

Granola and Labne

These days, many of us are considering making our own granola rather than buying it so that we can have a better idea of the quantity of sugar it contains. It's true that a bowl of oats and nuts bereft of spice and sugar can be boring so my recipe is both tasty and not too bad for you. I like to serve my granola with labne, a strained Lebanese yoghurt that is thick and creamy and in no way low fat, but you can use low-fat yoghurt if you like – but do check how much sugar is in the yoghurt as sugar is often added when the fat is taken out!

Makes 1kg of granola

For the labne

500g Greek yoghurt

pinch of salt

For the granola

450g rolled oats

200g bran flakes

150g almonds, coarsely chopped

100g mixed nuts, chopped

125g sunflower seeds

50g untoasted sesame seeds

120g light brown sugar

1 teaspoon sea salt

2 teaspoons ground cinnamon

3 teaspoons ground ginger

200g mixed dried fruit, roughly chopped

100ml maple syrup

50g clear honey

50g golden syrup

10ml vegetable oil

Make the labne the night before

Mix the yoghurt and salt well. Place in a non-reactive colander lined with muslin and rest over a bowl. Leave in the fridge overnight.

The next day, make the granola

Heat the oven to 150°C/gas 2.

In a large bowl, mix the oats, bran, nuts, seeds, sugar, salt and spices. Now add the dried fruit and mix again.

In a small saucepan, warm the maple syrup, honey and golden syrup with the vegetable oil.

Dribble the warm liquid into the dry mix, stirring all the time. Spread the mixture evenly over two baking sheets.

Bake for 40 minutes, until golden brown, stirring every 10 minutes, so it doesn't clump up too much – have some clumps but no big lumps. Take out the oven, and leave the granola to cool completely on the baking sheets.

Store in a big glass jar in your cupboard and marvel at how clever and healthy you are. Serve in a bowl with labne.

Corncakes and Smashed Avo (Sydneysider)

Breakfast is big in Sydney; it always has been and always will be. The chortle of young children asking for smashed avo in their best Aussie accent, the rumble of the coffee machine and scraping of chairs in a Sydney café always make me smile and I realise why I love the place. This is a two-parter; use the two things together for brunch or separately with other things.

A feast for 6*

For the corncakes

50g butter, melted and allowed to cool slightly

2 eggs, beaten

175ml milk

1 x 340g tin sweetcorn, drained

1 x 400g tin creamed corn

270g self-raising flour

1 teaspoon paprika

1 teaspoon bicarbonate of soda

2 teaspoons olive oil

12 rashers of smoked streaky bacon

salt and freshly ground black pepper

For the smashed avo

2–3 large ripe avocados

juice of ½ lemon

juice of 1 lime

2 drops of Tabasco sauce

To make the corncakes

Mix the butter with the eggs and milk, then add both lots of corn. In another bowl mix all the dry ingredients and season well. Combine the two mixes and stir until there are no flour lumps – it won't take long.

Put a heavy-based frying pan over a medium heat, add the oil and the bacon and cook the bacon for a couple of minutes until some is a little crispy but some isn't – I like the different textures. Take the bacon out of the pan but leave the oil (this is to fry the corncakes).

I use a tablespoon of mixture for each cake, simply spooning a few into the pan at a time depending on how big the pan is. Cook them over a medium heat, making sure the pan doesn't get too hot (if it does you'll start to smell the oil burning), until they start to puff up. Turn them over when the edges are brown, cook for another minute or so on the other side and repeat until they are all cooked. You should have a good 18–20 little corncakes for the hordes to feast on. You can keep them warm in the oven if you like but I don't think you need to as they cook pretty quick.

To smash an avo

Cut the avocados in half lengthways. Take out the seeds and keep one. Score the flesh in a criss-cross pattern all the way through to the skin, then gently squeeze the avo to release the cubes. Use a spoon to scoop all the bits out.

Using a fork, mash the flesh very well then add both types of juice and the Tabasco sauce then season.

If you're not using it straight away, store the avo in the fridge, covered with cling film and with the seed in the mix so it doesn't go grey.

* if there are fewer of you have leftovers the next day or in a couple of days' time

NB
You cannot smash an unripe avo!

American Pancakes

The standard weekend morning conversation in the Torode house centres around pancakes. Should they be thick or thin? Big, soft, thick, bouncy pancakes or paper-thin crêpes? With blueberries or served naked? The thing is, we all have our favourites and these are mine.

This is a basic batter and you can add stuff to the pancakes once they're in the pan. If you want to make flavoured pancakes, such as blueberry, chocolate, nuts or apple and cinnamon, just sprinkle them on top as the pancakes start to cook, don't mix them into the batter or the fruit prevents it cooking and the pancakes fall apart.

Makes 10 side-plate-sized pancakes

350g self-raising flour

1 teaspoon bicabarbonate of soda

½ teaspoon salt

1 teaspoon granulated sugar

100g butter

400ml milk

200ml buttermilk

2 eggs, beaten

50ml vegetable oil, for greasing

In a large bowl mix all the dry ingredients. Melt the butter and put to one side to cool slightly.

Now add all the wet ingredients (except the oil) to the dry ingredients, butter last, and give it a good beat with a whisk (balloon or electric). The batter should be smooth and silky and thick. Leave it to sit for 10 minutes to allow the bicarb to activate and start to bubble.

Warm your frying pan over a medium heat. Use a piece of kitchen paper to rub a little oil over the pan, just to grease it.

Pour a ladle of the batter into the centre of the pan. Now is the time to sprinkle over any flavourings if you are using them (see below). Leave the pancake to cook for a minute or so – bubbles will start to form in the batter but if they're surfacing very quickly the heat might be too high and you need to turn it down – you shouldn't be smelling any burning! When the edges are brown and the bubbles are popping (like the top of a crumpet) turn the pancake over and cook for a minute on the other side.

Continue to cook the pancakes, greasing the pan between each one if necessary, until you have cooked the lot. Make sure you keep a pancake for yourself as they disappear fast.

Pimp your pancakes…

Sprinkle over chocolate chips and walnuts, blueberries or blackberries, or whatever else you fancy at the point suggested above.

Once cooked, top them with bacon and maple syrup or cooked apples and cinnamon.

Posh French Toast

French toast, eggy bread... I don't mind what you call it but these hunks of egg-soaked sweetness are altogether very different from your standard take on the classic. You could stuff these pockets with whatever you want, but I think the combination here works and is definitely a crowd-pleaser. This is a very decadent breakfast or brunch but with chocolate sauce it could also be a dessert.

Makes 4

1 white farmhouse loaf, unsliced

2 bananas, halved lengthways

3 eggs, beaten

50ml buttermilk

pinch of salt

1 teaspoon cinnamon

2 teaspoons sugar

50g butter

30ml vegetable oil

Cut the bread into 5cm-thick slices and trim off the crusts. Cut an incision into the side of each slice of bread to make a pocket. Stuff a banana half into each pocket then squash the bread down with your hand. Be gentle but firm so that the bread doesn't split.

Mix the eggs with the buttermilk, salt, cinnamon and sugar and pour into a shallow dish or tray. Put two of the stuffed breads into the milk mix and leave to soak for 10 seconds, then turn and leave for another 10 seconds.

Heat a large frying pan over a medium heat, add some butter and a little oil. When the butter has melted and starts to sizzle, gently place the two pieces of soaked bread in the pan. Cook each side slowly, adjusting the heat so the bread lightly browns and smells of buttery toast. This will take a couple of minutes on each side.

Lift out of the pan, wipe the pan out and repeat with the other two pieces, adding more butter and oil. The first batch will stay warm.

Slice each piece of toast in half and serve.

Top with...

Whatever you like – some crème fraîche and maybe some maple syrup are good.

Baked Eggs, Spinach and Ham

Few recipes are original – this one definitely isn't – but by golly it's good. Baked eggs, or 'oeufs en cocotte', if you're French, have been around for years. They're really tasty and not difficult to make. It will take about 20 minutes to make these eggs from scratch but most of this time you have nothing to do because they're in the oven. A lazy breakfast can only ever be a good thing.

Feeds 4

240ml double cream

80g young spinach

8 eggs

3 slices of smoked York ham, roughly torn into pieces

salt and freshly ground black pepper

You will need four small frying pans or heatproof oval/round gratin dishes (sur le plat dishes, if you're being fancy)

Heat the oven to 220°C/gas 7.

Pour 60ml of cream into each dish and season well with salt and pepper. Place the dishes on a baking sheet and pop them in the oven for 5 minutes or until the cream is bubbling. Take the dishes out of the oven and turn the oven down to 200°C/gas 6.

Divide the spinach between the four dishes and give it a little stir, then crack two eggs into each dish on top of the spinach.

Place the dishes back in the oven and bake for 6–8 minutes – the egg whites should be cooked but the yolks still soft. Cook for longer if you like your eggs cooked more.

Divide the ham between the dishes and serve. Ham and eggs… Easy.

Or try…

Smoked salmon or trout, chopped tomatoes or chopped spicy sausage. Sprinkle with fresh chilli or cheese as they cook.

Omelette Arnold Bennett

An omelette is an omelette until it is a Bennett. And Mr Bennett had a good idea when it came to brunch: baked eggs with smoked haddock and white sauce, finished with lots of grated cheese. It's good, really good, and decadent.

My father used to say that a gentleman always eats well, even alone. This is my gentleman's breakfast.

Serves 2

200g smoked haddock

½ small onion, peeled

200ml milk

20g butter, plus extra for greasing

20g plain flour

6 eggs

200g Gruyère, grated

salt and freshly ground black pepper

Heat the oven to 200°C/gas 6. Butter one large or two small heatproof dishes.

Poach the haddock

Put the haddock and onion into a pan and season well. Pour over the milk and place over a medium heat. Bring the milk to the boil, then take the pan off the heat and leave it to stand for 10 minutes – this is enough time to cook the fish and flavour the milk for the sauce.

Carefully lift the fish and onion out of the milk, put the fish on a plate, discard the onion and pour the milk into a jug. Skin the fish and ditch the fish skin. Break the fish into large shards of flesh and set aside.

Make the white sauce

Melt the butter in the pan you used to poach the fish, then add the flour and stir to make a paste (it's called a roux). Whisk in the fish-infused milk, a little at a time, until it's become a sauce. Gently bring the sauce to the boil and cook for a couple of minutes until thickened. Slide the fish (along with any liquid on the plate) into the sauce, gently fold it in and then remove the pan from the heat.

Almost there...

Break the eggs into a large bowl, mix well and season a little with salt and pepper. Pour the eggs into the prepared dish or dishes, top with the haddock and white sauce mixture and cover with the grated cheese.

Slide the dishes onto a baking sheet and bake them in the oven for about 10 minutes, until puffed up. Heat the grill to high.

Remove the baking sheet and dishes from the oven and slide under the grill for a few minutes, until puffy and golden brown. Brunch ahoy!

Poached Eggs with Tomato Kasundi, Yoghurt and Coriander

Kasundi was introduced to me by a chef who I worked with when I first arrived in London. However, it was only very recently that I discovered it was not his invention as he proclaimed, but a classic Indian sauce. This ripper of a spicy sauce will last for a good week in the fridge but also freezes really well. And it's good with other things as well as poached eggs.

For 2

For the tomato kasundi

100ml malt vinegar

50g fresh root ginger, peeled and grated

5 garlic cloves, finely chopped

6 long green chillies, de-seeded, if you wish, and finely chopped

2 teaspoons ground turmeric

2 teaspoons cayenne pepper

80g soft brown sugar, plus extra for seasoning

25ml fish sauce, plus extra for seasoning

2 teaspoons cumin seeds, toasted then ground

50ml olive oil

2 teaspoons black mustard seeds

1kg tomatoes, skinned and chopped (see page 224)

For the poached eggs

50ml malt vinegar

4 eggs

To serve

100ml thick yoghurt

a handful of freshly chopped coriander

Make the kasundi

Put everything except the oil, mustard seeds and tomatoes into a food processor and blitz to a paste.

Take a decent size of saucepan and heat the olive oil over a medium heat and then drop in the mustard seeds. When they start to pop, add the paste, stir it all together and cook gently on a low heat for 10 minutes until bubbling and fragrant.

Drop the tomatoes into the cooked paste and cook for a further 20 minutes. Taste and season with a little more fish sauce and sugar.

Poach the eggs

Put the vinegar and 2 litres of water in a deep pan and bring to a rolling boil. Break the eggs into the pan at 12 o'clock, then 6 o'clock, then 3 o'clock and finally at 9 o'clock. You need to keep the water at a rolling boil as you add the eggs so keep turning up the heat as necessary. Once the eggs float to the surface, cook for a further 2 minutes.

To serve

Put a good layer of the kasundi sauce into two warmed bowls and top with two poached eggs. Add a spoonful of yoghurt and a sprinkling of coriander.

Green Eggs and Ham

Many of us grew up reading Dr. Seuss's story of Green Eggs and Ham. While on a trip to Australia and struggling with jet lag, I was taken for breakfast by my brother, overlooking Sydney's Manly Beach. I ordered a long black coffee with an extra shot to wake me up; he ordered green eggs and ham. I was dubious at first but it's simply ham with eggs and pesto on thick toast, so of course it works. 'I like them Sam-I-am, I like them green eggs and ham.'

For 2

4 large eggs

100ml double cream

30g butter, softened, plus extra to serve

1 tablespoon pesto

4 thick slices of bread (I like to use pumpernickel)

4 thick slices of smoked ham

salt and freshly ground black pepper

Break the eggs into a bowl and add the cream. Use a fork to stab at the eggs so the yolks break up but the eggs are not mixed up too much.

Heat the butter in a frying pan over a medium heat. Add the pesto, give it a good stir and then pour in the egg mixture and season, being careful not to add too much salt as pesto can be salty. Keep stirring the now green eggs until the eggs are starting to set. Take the pan off the heat and leave the eggs to stand for 2 minutes, then give them another stir – the eggs will be cooked all the way through but not dry.

Meanwhile, toast the bread, butter it, then top it with the ham. Spoon over the eggs and you're done.

Mushrooms on Toast

This is a good one for your vegetarian mates (I like to keep everyone happy). The cheese and mushrooms are woody, sweet and salty. Top this with an egg – fried or poached – should you feel that brunch is not brunch without one.

For 4

20ml extra virgin olive oil

1 small garlic clove, finely chopped

4 thick slices of sourdough bread or similar

50g unsalted butter

300g mixed wild mushrooms (chanterelles, ceps, morels etc.)

2 tablespoons white wine

a good handful of flat-leaf parsley, roughly chopped

100g fresh goat's cheese.

salt and freshly ground black pepper

Heat the oil in a large frying pan. Turn the heat down to medium, add the garlic and leave it to soften for a few minutes but don't let it brown.

Meanwhile, heat a griddle pan for the toast. (Or toast it in a minute).

Turn the heat up under the garlic and add half the butter to the pan. When the butter is sizzling and starts to turn brown add the mushrooms and stir, making sure that they are coated with garlic. Allow the mushrooms to brown slightly, then add the wine. Bring to the boil, and bubble it to reduce it until there is only a small amount of liquid left in the pan. Season with salt and plenty of pepper, stir in the parsley and put to one side.

On the preheated griddle, toast the bread for a minute or so on each side. Butter the toast and put the mushroom mixture on top. Spoon over a good blob of the goat's cheese and serve topped with a fried or poached egg – or not.

Mushroom and Horseradish Doughnuts

Savoury doughnuts, now there's a thing. I used to make these to sit alongside roast beef – that was until I discovered the great Yorkshire pudding (see page 117). I still serve them with a roast but also as a snack or at a party.

When you work with yeast, you need to think about the temperature. Yeast likes to be warm and cosy. Use your body as a temperature gauge – if it feels warm then it is working properly and the dough will be light and fluffy. Make variations of savoury doughnuts as starters, sides or just finger food. Happy Doughnuting!

Makes 24

1 x 7g sachet dried active yeast

10g caster sugar

30ml warm water

480g strong white flour, plus extra for dusting

50g dried milk powder

10g salt, plus extra for sprinkling

240ml milk

40g butter

2 eggs

50g dried porcini mushrooms, soaked then drained

3 litres vegetable oil, for deep-frying

100g creamed horseradish sauce

You will need a stand mixer fitted with a K hook for this

Make the dough

In a cup, mix the yeast and a pinch of sugar with the warm water. Stir so the yeast and sugar dissolve.

Put the flour and milk powder into your stand mixer bowl with the salt and the remaining sugar.

Warm the milk and butter in a small pan until you can just hold your finger in the milk. Turn off the heat. Crack your eggs into the warm buttery milk and beat them in, add the mushrooms, then pour in the yeast mixture. You now have a batch of wet mixture and a batch of dry mixture.

Turn the mixer on. Quickly pour the wet mixture into the dry mixture. Now leave the machine on a medium speed to knead the dough for 10 minutes until it is smooth and stretchy – the dough should be really sticky.

Rest it

Take the hook out the bowl, and cover the bowl with a clean tea towel. Leave it somewhere warm to prove for an hour, until doubled in size.

Slap the dough and it will deflate, like a balloon. Scrape the dough out of the bowl onto a lightly floured surface. Using a dough scraper or a butter knife, cut the dough into four and then divide each portion into six (it's easiest to work with it like this – you want 24 pieces in total). Roll each portion of dough into a ball and place on a floured tray, spaced apart. Cover the dough with oiled cling film and leave to rise again for about 45 minutes, until they've nearly doubled in size.

Almost there...

Mushroom and Horseradish Doughnuts

Cook the doughnuts

Take the cling film off the dough balls and using the palm of your hand, gently press down a little on each one so that it looks more like an ice hockey puck than a ball.

Pour the vegetable oil into a deep pan (or use a deep fat fryer) and heat the oil to 170°C.

Fry the doughnuts, six at a time, for 3–4 minutes each side, turning the doughnuts with a slotted spoon as they bob around the surface, until the doughnuts are golden brown on each side. Lift the doughnuts out of the oil.

Fill them

Spoon the creamed horseradish into a piping bag fitted with a little nozzle. Push the nozzle into the centre of each ball and pipe a little horseradish inside. Sprinkle the doughnuts with a little salt (or you could even use some chicken salt). Doughnuts... yum!

Toasted Banana Bread

Toasted banana bread is a stalwart for brekkie in Australia and sits on nearly every café menu and blackboard. It is always toasted and always served with loads of butter. It's simple and yum!

Makes 1 loaf

4 very ripe bananas

120g butter or margarine, softened, plus extra for greasing

90g caster sugar

90g soft light brown sugar

2 eggs, beaten

240g self-raising flour

40g wholemeal flour

1 teaspoon ground cinnamon

1 tablespoon clear honey

1 tablespoon maple syrup

For the maple butter

100g butter, softened

2 tablespoons maple syrup

Heat the oven to 180°C/gas 4. Grease a 900g loaf tin.

In a large bowl, mash the bananas really well with a fork.

In a separate large bowl, beat the butter and sugars until light and fluffy, then mix in the eggs. Add the mashed bananas and mix again. Stir in the flours and cinnamon and then the honey and maple syrup.

Scrape the mixture into the tin and bake for 30 minutes, then lower the heat to 150°C/gas 2 and bake for a further 10 minutes, until golden brown and a skewer inserted into the centre comes out clean.

Meanwhile. make the maple butter. Whip the butter with a balloon whisk until it's white and fluffy, then whisk in the maple syrup.

Turn the bread out onto a wire rack and try to leave it to cool. You can eat the bread as it is, toast it under a grill, or I fry mine in a dry pan and spread it with lashings of maple butter.

Hot Bacon and Gruyère Breakfast Bread

This delicious bread can be made the night before and baked first thing in the morning or you can bake it then reheat it the next day, spraying it with a little water before it goes in the oven. Hot it is addictive, so make lots; but cold it's just as good, so make double lots. I think you need to use a mixer rather than your hands to make this bread – it's really quick and easy that way.

Makes 12 pieces*

1 teaspoon olive oil, plus extra for greasing

1 x 7g sachet dried active yeast

1 tablespoon milk, plus extra for brushing

350ml water (body temperature, not cold, please)

sprinkle of sugar

500g strong white flour, plus extra for dusting

10g salt

80g butter, cut into chunks plus 75g butter, melted

300g lardons, cooked with black pepper (see page 46, if you need some pointers on cooking your bacon)

200g Gruyère, roughly chopped

1 x 100g block mozzarella, grated

2 handfuls of chopped mixed fresh herbs, such as basil, chives, sage, oregano and parsley

a handful of grated Parmesan

* depending on how you tear it apart!

To make the dough

Grease a 28cm ring mould or savarin tin with oil.

Mix the yeast with the milk, oil and a couple of teaspoons of the water, plus a sprinkle of sugar. Leave somewhere warm for 10 minutes until it starts to bubble – the bubbles mean the yeast is working.

Put the flour and salt into your stand mixer bowl and mix well. Mix the bubbling yeast mix with the rest of the water and add this to the flour.

Start the mixer on a slow speed, then increase and beat the dough for a good 8–10 minutes. It's had enough time when it is slapping the sides of the bowl – you will see/hear what I mean. Add the butter and beat again for 1 minute.

If you don't have a mixer, just be prepared to work your arm muscles hard.

Leave it to rest

Now you have to be a little patient. Leave the dough in a warm place, covered with a tea towel, to rise for 30 minutes – it will double in size.

Once the dough has risen, beat it again to knock out the air and lift it out of the mixer bowl. Lightly flour your work surface and roll the dough into a log about 30cm long and slice it into 12 pieces.

Roll each piece into a ball and then flatten slightly. Stick a good amount of bacon, cheese and herbs in the middle of each one and fold the dough over to wrap them. Coat each of the dough balls in melted butter then roll in grated parmesan. Lay all the filled dough balls in the tin. Drape some oiled cling film over the tin and put the whole lot in the fridge overnight.

Almost there...

Hot Bacon and Gruyère Breakfast Bread

...from the previous page

To bake the bread

In the morning, heat the oven to 200°C/gas 6.

Put the bread in the oven, then immediately turn it down to 180°C/gas 4 and bake for 40 minutes, until golden brown.

Leave to cool a little before serving, but not long, and whatever you do, don't turn your back or it will all be gone!

Quick, turn the page again to see it go...

You can also

Add some French mustard to the cheese.

Once the bread is cold, make a great savoury bread and butter pudding with horseradish.

Hash Browns, Crispy Bacon and Fried Egg

As a youngster I was taken to America on holiday by my dad. It was 4th July 1974, and our first day in San Francisco, when I sat and watched a man make hash browns. My brothers and I named the owner and the waitress Cranky Frankie and Nervous Nora. Frankie was the cook and Nora was always getting things wrong and Frankie was always shouting. The food, however, was delicious; the hash browns my favourite.

Enough for 4*

4 teaspoons vegetable oil, plus extra if necessary

12 rashers of smoked streaky bacon

1 small onion, grated

30g butter, melted

3 large baking potatoes, baked and peeled

2 tablespoons olive oil

4 large eggs

salt and freshly ground black pepper

* This recipe should make 8–10 hash browns and you only need eight to serve, so any extras are yours to eat. You're the cook – it's testing, yes testing.

Heat the oven to 180°C/gas 4 and put a baking sheet in the oven to heat up.

Fry the bacon

Put the vegetable oil and bacon in a cold frying pan and place the pan over a low heat. Slowly cook the bacon so the fat comes out. Turn it a few times and when it is starting to go crispy take the pan off the heat and take the bacon out but leave the fat.

Make the hash browns

Mix the butter with the grated onion and season. Coarsely grate the potato and mix it with the onion really thoroughly. Roll the mixture into golf-ball-sized pieces and then flatten them to the thickness of your thumb. I like individual hash browns as I like the crispy bits.

Reheat the bacon pan and pop the hash browns in. Cook over a low heat until they start to colour round the edges. Once they start to brown, turn them over and cook for another minute or so. Now turn the heat up and they'll start to sizzle. Turn them again for another minute and they'll turn crispy.

Pop the hash browns on the heated baking sheet, along with the bacon, and put them into the oven to keep warm.

Fry the eggs

Wipe out the frying pan, add the olive oil and when the pan is hottish crack in the eggs. I like the edges of my eggs crispy so I keep the heat high and the eggs will splutter, but it's your call. Cook yours how you like them.

Bingo, American-style brekkie

Dish out the hash browns and the bacon and lay the eggs over the top. I like mine with Tabasco and tomato sauce but it's up to you.

Cowboy Breakfast

This should probably be called the student or the single-pan breakfast. It got its name because everything is cooked in one pan as cowboys would have had to do. Where they would have found sausages and bacon and eggs on the prairie I don't quite know but I like the idea. This is my *Brokeback Mountain*.

Feeds 2–4

4 sausages

20ml vegetable oil

4 rashers of smoked streaky bacon

2 tomatoes, halved

2 flat mushrooms

20g butter

4 eggs

freshly ground black pepper

Heat a large frying pan over a medium heat. Add the sausages and oil, and fry the sausages, turning them regularly, until they have some colour.

Drop in the bacon, and add the tomatoes, cut-side down, then season everything with a good grind of pepper. Keep turning the sausages and the bacon but leave the tomatoes undisturbed, until the sausages and bacon are cooked through.

Push the sausages and bacon to one side of the pan, add the mushrooms and butter and let them sizzle. Cook the mushrooms, open-side down, for a few minutes, then turn them over and turn over the tomatoes at the same time.

Now spread everything around the pan, making sure there is a bit of everything in each quarter. If necessary, carefully drain off any excess fat so it's not greasy. Break the eggs into the pan and let them cook, until fried to your liking. Grab a bottle of tomato sauce and some toast and you're ready to eat. Yee-hah!

Stewed Plums with Spiced Yoghurt

Stewed fruit for brunch is a must, either served on its own, with yoghurt or on pancakes or French toast. I like to serve these plump vanilla-y discs of loveliness with cinnamon, be it in the yoghurt or with/on/over any of the other breakfast goodies you choose to serve them with.

Enough for 8*

600g plums

475g caster sugar

2 vanilla pods, split lengthways

200ml Greek yoghurt

2 teaspoons ground cinnamon

* the plums can be stored for ages and used as you need them

Bring a large pot of water to the boil. Prick the skins of the plums and drop them into the boiling water for 30 seconds, just to blister the skin. Drain in a colander, then when they're cool enough to handle, carefully peel the skins and throw them away. Cut the plums in half, twist them so that one side comes free and dig the stone out of the other half with a teaspoon.

Put the sugar, plums and the split vanilla in the pan and cover with warm water. Bring to the boil, then turn the heat down so that it simmers for about 15 minutes, until soft. Gently lift the plums out of the liquid into a bowl while you reduce the cooking liquid. Bubble the cooking liquid until it is a syrup but is not too sticky. Drop the plums back into the pan to coat them in the syrup and store any you don't use in sterilised jars.

Mix the yoghurt with a little of the cooled syrup and the cinnamon. Serve, eat and enjoy.

My On-the-run Breakfast Bars

Now that I cycle a lot more and also commute long distances on my trusty bike, I don't want a heavy breakfast before clipping into the pedals. So I designed these little beauties to eat while riding and also to refuel at the end of a long ride. I'm sure many of you are in a rush mid-week and these will be enough to keep you going for a good few hours should you be too busy to grab some brekkie before rushing out of the door.

Makes about 24

75g butter, plus extra for greasing

100ml maple syrup

50g golden syrup

50g treacle

100g dates, roughly chopped

100g soft prunes, roughly chopped

100g granola (shop-bought or see page 18)

100g porridge oats

60g dried apples, roughly chopped

60g dried figs, roughly chopped

60g dried mango, roughly chopped

60g sultanas, roughly chopped

60g raisins, roughly chopped

60g dried mixed fruit

50g dried milk powder

6 sheets of edible rice paper

Heat the oven to 180°C/gas 4. Grease a 30 x 20 x 3cm brownie tin.

Put the butter, syrups, treacle, dates and prunes in a large pan. Bring to the boil and mash the fruit as well as you can with a fork. Take off the heat and leave to cool a little.

Put all the remaining ingredients, except for the rice paper, into a large mixing bowl and stir well. Keep mixing as you pour in the syrup and fruit mixture and continue to mix until it is all sticky.

Line the base of the brownie tin with half the rice paper. Cover it with the mixture and spread it out evenly so the top is flat. Bake in the oven for 15 minutes, until dark and soggy, then take it out and press the other sheet of rice paper onto the top while it's still hot. Turn out onto a wire rack and allow to cool completely.

Cut into long bars and bingo … you are set. Store the bars in a lidded cake tin for up to a couple of weeks (if they last that long).

Although I am a professional cook, there are certain dishes I rely on time and again when cooking at home. Some are posh, some are simple but all are favourites.

for the family

Pizza Bianca or Not

Pizza is good. There's the classic with tomato sauce and a scattering of toppings like mozzarella, olives, anchovies or ham; and then there's 'pizza bianca', where the base is just smothered with crème fraîche – no tomato, no cheese.

Here the dough's the recipe and I've given you a couple of topping suggestions; the rest is up to you. Let children make theirs and then make something a bit more grown up for you – or not, depending on your inner child. If you are my daughter pizza means making a pig face with whatever toppings you like.

Makes 4 pizzas

For the dough

275ml warm water

1 x 7g sachet dried active yeast

½ teaspoon sugar

375g '00' flour, plus extra for dusting

1 teaspoon salt

1 tablespoon olive oil, plus extra for oiling

For a pizza bianca

200ml crème fraîche

200g Parma ham, thinly sliced

For a classic tomato base

1 x 400ml tin chopped tomatoes

300g mozzarella

salt and freshly ground black pepper

You will need a stand mixer fitted with a dough hook

To make the dough

Mix together the water, yeast and sugar and leave to sit for 10 minutes.

Place half the flour in the bowl of a stand mixer fitted with a dough hook and pour in the liquid. Beat on a medium speed for 10 minutes then leave to stand somewhere warm for about 10 minutes, until foamy. Add the remaining flour, the salt and olive oil and beat the dough for a further 5 minutes, until it's a puffy white ball.

Sit the dough in a well-oiled bowl, cover with a tea towel and leave somewhere warm for about 30 minutes or until the dough has doubled in size.

Slap the dough down and knead on a floured worktop for a few minutes, until soft but not too elastic Divide the dough into four pieces, roll into balls and leave to rest for 10 minutes.

If you're having a tomato base...

Empty the tin of tomatoes into a small saucepan. Bring to the boil and season well. Cook for 5–10 minutes, or until it's the consistency you'd like, then take off the heat and allow to cool.

Almost there...

Pizza Bianca or Not

...from the previous page

To finish and bake

Heat the oven to the highest temperature possible. Place a baking sheet in the oven so that it gets very hot.

With a well-floured rolling pin, flatten each ball of dough and roll it out as thin as possible. Remove the baking sheet from the oven and dust it with a little flour. Rub the tiniest amount of oil on one side of one pizza base and flip it over onto the floured baking sheet.

For a pizza bianca smear a quarter of the crème fraîche over the dough.

For a classic tomato version do the same with some of your tomato sauce. Tear some of the mozzarella and scatter it over the top.

Slide the baking sheet onto the top shelf of your very hot oven and cook for 5–6 minutes, until the pizza is brown and crispy around the edges. Repeat until all the pizzas are cooked.

Arrange the Parma ham on the pizza bianca along with any other toppings you like, and either eat the tomato version as it is or add your toppings.

Posh toppings for grown-ups (or adventurous children)

Bresaola, shaved fennel, anchovies and capers, grated Parmesan and roasted peppers or maybe even pepperoni.

Leek and Mushroom Pithivier

Creamed leeks are one of my favourite roast dinner sides and are the inspiration behind this 'pithivier', which is a smart French pie decorated with a Catherine wheel pattern of markings on top. Please let the filling cool down before you build the pie to guarantee the pastry is crispy and flaky. It makes a great light lunch or first course and can be made in advance then kept in the fridge for a couple of days until you are ready to bake it.

Feeds 8–10

125g unsalted butter, plus extra for greasing

6 leeks, green parts discarded, the rest washed and chopped

150ml crème fraîche

200g button mushrooms, sliced

plain flour, for dusting

500g puff pastry (I like the blocks you can roll out)

200g Gruyère, cut into chunks

egg glaze (1 egg yolk beaten with 1 teaspoon water)

salt and freshly ground black pepper

For the filling

Melt 25g of the butter in a heavy-based pan over a medium heat. Add the leeks and cook, stirring frequently, for about 2 minutes. Add another 40g of butter and 3 tablespoons of water, cover with a lid, reduce the heat to low and cook the leeks, stirring occasionally, for 20 minutes, or until tender. Uncover the pan and continue to cook for 5–7 minutes, until all the moisture has evaporated. Transfer to a large bowl and leave to cool.

When cool, add the crème fraîche and place in the fridge until cold.

Melt the remaining butter in a frying pan over a high heat. Add the mushrooms and cook, tossing frequently, for about 5 minutes, until they are lightly browned. Season to taste. Add the mushrooms to the leeks and stir gently so that the pieces of leek keep their shape.

Heat the oven to 200°C/gas 6. Grease a sheet of greaseproof paper.

To build the pithivier

On a lightly floured worktop, roll out one half of the pastry into a 25cm round. Slide the pastry onto the greased paper and place on a baking sheet.

Leaving a 2.5cm margin all around the edge, spread half the leek mixture over the pastry. Put the Gruyère in the centre then top with the rest of the leek mixture. The cheese will melt in the middle.

Roll out the remaining pastry into a 33cm round. This will be the pie lid so it needs to be slighter larger than the first round.

Brush the pastry margin around the leeks with some of the egg glaze. Place the pastry lid over the top and use the back of a fork to crimp around the edge to seal the pie. Trim away any excess pastry. Brush the pie with the remaining glaze, then roll the back of a knife over the top of the pastry to score it with curved lines.

Place the pie in the oven on the lowest oven shelf and bake for 15 minutes, then turn the oven down to 180°C/gas 4 and bake for a further 30 minutes, until golden brown and crisp.

Take the pie out of the oven and leave to sit for about 10 minutes before you cut it up and eat it.

Roasted Root Vegetable Salad

I adore winter and autumn root vegetables, simply roasted, well seasoned and just served piled up on a big plate, all honest and sweet and earthy. This is a bung-it-all-in recipe. You can posh it up with some herbs or curd cheese or even anchovies, but on their own the veg are just great. Eat hot or cold.

Feeds 6–8

2 red onions, quartered

½ small butternut squash, peeled, de-seeded and cut into chunks about the same size as the onions

1 large red pepper, cut into 8 cubes

12 new potatoes or small salad potatoes

4 small parsnips, halved lengthways

4 carrots, halved lengthways

60ml vegetable oil

3 garlic cloves, crushed

1 small bag of pea shoots or watercress

salt and freshly ground black pepper

For the dressing

4 teaspoons olive oil

4 teaspoons red wine vinegar

The veg

Heat the oven to 220°C/gas 7.

Put the onion, squash, red pepper, potatoes, parsnips and carrots in a large bowl. Add the vegetable oil, garlic and a good amount of salt and pepper and mix really well so all the vegetables are coated and seasoned.

Tip the vegetables into a roasting tin and spread out. Roast in the oven for 30 minutes (do not move the veg while they are roasting). Give the tin a shake and cook for a further 15 minutes until they've got crispy bits. Take out of the oven and transfer the veg to a salad bowl.

The dressing

To make the dressing, pour the olive oil and vinegar into the roasting tin and stir. Pour this dressing over the warm vegetables and scatter over the pea shoots or watercress.

Or you can...

Change the combination of veg to suit what you like and what's around. Add blanched beans, peas, asparagus, pumpkin seeds, pine nuts or any other nice things.

Polenta with Blue Cheese and Mushrooms

I love polenta served creamy and fluffy and cheesy. It needs to be wet in the same way as porridge needs to be wet; not enough liquid and it can be a little solid. To make the polenta a big plate of loveliness, just add the mushrooms and some blue cheese and bingo, it's a beaut!

Feeds 4–6

For the polenta

300ml milk

200ml water

½ teaspoon salt

¼ teaspoon ground black pepper

1 garlic clove, smashed with the back of a knife then peeled

100g polenta

120ml double cream

20g Parmesan, grated

70g mascarpone cheese

For the mushrooms and cheese

2 teaspoons olive oil

10g butter

1 large shallot, diced

200g mixed wild mushrooms, wiped clean with a damp cloth

2 tablespoons crème fraîche

a handful of flat-leaf parsley, chopped

150g creamy blue cheese, such as Gorgonzola or similar

salt and freshly ground black pepper

The polenta

Put the milk, water, salt, pepper and garlic in a large pan and bring to a rolling boil. Add the polenta, stirring all the time, and continue to stir until it returns to the boil. Turn it down and cook over a low heat for 15 minutes and keep stirring. Add the cream and Parmesan and cook for about 2 minutes, but keep stirring until the cheese has melted. Take off the heat and beat in the mascarpone. It will stay warm while you sort out the rest.

The mushrooms

Put the olive oil, butter and shallot in a frying pan over a medium heat and sweat the shallot until transparent. Add the mushrooms, season well and cook for 2 minutes, don't move them or they go soggy. Now turn the mushrooms over, add the crème fraîche and bring to the boil.

The cheese

Dish up as you like – in a big plate or individual plates. Spoon the mushrooms over the polenta, sprinkle with the parsley and then crumble over the blue cheese.

Baked Tofu and Yummy Veggies Inside

Please give this recipe a go, especially if you have never eaten tofu before. It's tasty and gutsy and full of chilli spice – do add more spice if you like. The aubergines are cooked in a way that means they will never be greasy. The tofu pockets may split a little but that's okay – just pile the saucy aubergines over the top with real generosity.

For 4 people to feast on*

2 large aubergines, sliced into eighths lengthways

50ml vegetable oil, plus extra for greasing

2 tablespoons black bean sauce

2 long red chillies, sliced

60g spring onions

700g firm tofu

*or a side dish for 6

Heat the oven to 200°C/gas 6.

Steam or boil the aubergines in a pan until they are light grey in colour. Drain well. (Boiling the aubergines before you fry them means that they won't absorb too much oil.)

Heat the oil in a large frying pan. Drop the aubergines into the pan and leave to cook until coloured, then gently turn over and cook the other side – about 4–5 minutes. Add the black bean sauce, 3 tablespoons of water and the chillies. Toss the aubergines and then stir in the spring onions. Take off the heat and leave to cool a little.

Cut the tofu into blocks about the size of a deck of cards. Carefully cut an incision in the side of each block to make a pocket, then fill each with a good amount of the aubergine mixture. Don't worry if they split a little bit.

Place the stuffed tofu in a roasting tin and bake for 20 minutes or until coloured and bubbling.

Serve with any aubergine that didn't fit into the tofu and maybe a cup of miso soup or a glass of red wine.

Change the filling

Tofu can be stuffed with anything: try a little crab or spicy mince or maybe a pile of shredded vegetables or leftover curry, or even Bolognese sauce (see my Sloppy Joe Bolognese on page 108).

Spiced Butternut Squash Noodles

Many moons ago a group of friends were coming for dinner and I had promised them a chicken Thai curry, only to find one of them didn't eat chicken. The plan had to change and this noodle dish was born. It is proper fusion food, with bits and pieces from all over the globe. I still love it and make it whenever I can. The lime pickle was a last-minute addition because I wanted the dish to be spicy, sharp and sour. It worked.

Feeds 6

1 butternut squash

80ml vegetable oil

100g Thai red curry paste (bought or see my recipe on page 102)

30g palm sugar (or soft brown sugar is just as good)

2 x 400ml tins coconut milk

175ml coconut cream

1 tablespoon Thai fish sauce

3 tablespoons hot Indian lime pickle

3 lemongrass stalks, bashed

200ml water

500g egg noodles, pre-cooked

100g beansprouts

good-sized bunch of coriander, leaves picked

Peel the butternut squash, remove the seeds, then cut into 4–5cm chunks.

Heat the oil in a wok over a medium heat. Add the red curry paste and fry and stir for 2 minutes, then add the palm sugar and let it cook, stirring all the time, until it becomes almost volcanic, sticky and fragrant – this makes a richer and sweeter curry.

Add the squash, stir and coat with the paste, then pour in the coconut milk. Add the coconut cream, fish sauce, lime pickle and lemongrass. Bring to the boil, add the water, and simmer for about 20 minutes, until the squash is soft but not mushy.

Put the noodles into a large bowl and pour boiling water over them to heat them up. Leave for a couple of minutes, then drain well.

Divide the noodles between bowls and ladle over your butternut squash mix, top with beansprouts, coriander and maybe a bit more sauce for luck.

My Fish Fingers

It is not unusual to be eating fish fingers in the Torode household and it will invariably be these ones. Mine*; my crisp polenta-crusted fingers, served with pickles and white bread, to make a sandwich – or not. These have all the comfort a fish finger should have.

Feeds 4–6

4 pieces of thick cod or haddock, each about the size of your hand (225–250g per piece)

100g plain flour

100g polenta

100g fine dry breadcrumbs

2 eggs, beaten with a little milk

500ml vegetable oil, for frying

salt and freshly ground black pepper

To make and coat

Skin the fish. Now turn it so that the sloping edges of the fish are facing you head on, this will allow you to cut against the grain – if you don't the fish will fall apart as it cooks. Cut each piece of fish into four thick strips – they will be bigger than shop-bought fish fingers.

Put the flour on a plate and season well. Mix the polenta and breadcrumbs together in a shallow dish. Pour the egg mixture into another. Line up the dishes in front of you with the flour first and the polenta last.

Roll each fish finger in the flour, dip it in the egg mixture, then lift it out and let the excess egg drain off. Finally, roll the fish in the polenta breadcrumbs. Make sure each finger is well coated and the crumbs are patted down. Repeat until you have coated all the fingers.

To cook

Heat the oil in a deep, large frying pan until it reaches 180°C and is shimmering. Gently lay a few of the fish fingers in the oil, but don't overcrowd the pan or the oil temperature will drop and the fingers won't be crispy. Fry the fingers until golden brown underneath, then carefully turn over and gently fry the other sides until golden. The fish will be cooked through. Repeat until all the fish fingers are cooked.

* You'll see them on the next page...

Serve with...

Fresh white bread, tomato sauce, vinegar, lemon wedges...
Fish finger sandwiches = joy of joys.

Fishcakes

What do you give a fish on its birthday? A fish cake. I know, I am terrible at telling jokes. Best I stick to the cooking! These fishcakes are big and hearty and chunky. I like fishcakes that have a crunchy outside with big bits of fish and loads of potato and herbs. Make them as big as mine or smaller if you want.

Makes 6 good-sized fishcakes

2 big floury baking potatoes, about 600g in total

250g salmon fillet, skin on

250g cod fillet, skin on

200g undyed smoked haddock

2 litres boiling water

50ml white wine vinegar

1 small red onion, very finely diced

1 long red chilli, de-seeded and diced

a good handful of chopped flat-leaf parsley

a good handful of chopped coriander

25g butter

finely grated zest and juice of ½ lemon

1 egg, beaten

50g plain flour, for coating

100m vegetable oil, for frying

salt and freshly ground black pepper

Heat the oven to 200°C/gas 6 and bake the potatoes for 45–50 minutes, or until soft. (Leave the oven on.)

Meanwhile, put all the fish in a large pan. Pour over the boiling water, add the vinegar, a teaspoon of salt and some pepper. Bring to the boil, then turn off the heat and leave the fish to sit in the water for 10 minutes.

Take the fish out of the pan and put it on a board. Turn it skin-side up, peel off the skin and get rid of it. To break up the fish, just push each fillet down gently and it will naturally break into big chunks.

Put the onion, chilli and herbs in a large bowl and drop in the fish.

Peel the potatoes while still warm and crush them with a fork into chunks about the same size as the fish chunks. Put the potato in a separate bowl and drop in the butter, lemon zest and juice and stir well.

Gently mix the fish and potato together, trying to keep it chunky. Divide the mix in half and then each half into three. Roll each bundle of fish into a ball and then shape into a fishcake.

Put the egg into a shallow bowl and the flour on a plate. Dip each fishcake first in the beaten egg and then in the flour. Make sure they're coated all over.

Heat the oil in a large frying pan and fry the fishcakes, in batches if necessary, over a medium heat until golden brown on each side – roughly 5 minutes per side.

Put the fishcakes onto a baking sheet and bake in the oven for 5 minutes or until they are hot all the way through.

Freeze them

The fishcakes freeze really well once fried. Make as above, but leave to cool after frying them and then freeze. Defrost in the fridge overnight and then bake in an oven heated to 200°C/gas 6 for about 20 minutes. Done.

Indonesian Fish Curry with Clams, Mussels and Beansprouts

This is a proper treat, a pot of spiced deliciousness. It's not cheap, I know, but it really is a worthwhile big bowl of fun and flavour. It will feed a big family and as many friends that you can get around the table. Let people serve themselves with as much or as little of the shells as they like.

Feeds a big family

50ml vegetable oil

3 tablespoons Thai red curry paste (bought or see page 102)

1 teaspoon paprika

2 x 400ml tins coconut milk, left in the fridge overnight

200ml water

10 fresh kaffir lime leaves

10 fresh curry leaves

200g clams, cleaned

200g mussels, cleaned

1kg skinned white fish, such as cod, pollock and haddock, cut into 5cm chunks

12 large prawns

1½ teaspoons salt

a handful of cherry tomatoes, quartered

2½ tablespoons lime juice

To serve

150g beansprouts

a handful of mint leaves

Get the curry going

Heat the oil in a wok, add the red curry paste and paprika, stir and cook for a couple of minutes over a high heat. Add 100ml of the coconut milk, stir and cook on a lower heat for 5 minutes. Add the remaining coconut milk, the water, lime leaves and curry leaves and bring to the boil. Reduce the heat and simmer for 10 minutes until thickened and creamy, then remove from the heat.

Cook the clams and mussels

Cook the clams and the mussels separately. Put about 100ml of the sauce into a large pan, add the clams and bring to the boil, then cover with the lid and cook for about 4–5 minutes over a high heat until all the shells have opened (throw away any shells that are broken or do not open – these are bad for you). Repeat with the mussels.

Finish

Bring the wok with the remaining sauce to the boil, drop in the fish and prawns along with the salt and tomatoes. When it comes to a simmer, take it off the heat, give it a good stir and add the lime juice. Put the beansprouts and mint leaves into the base of individual bowls and pour over the curry. The beansprouts will cook and all the flavour in the mint will be released. Keep the clams and mussels separate for everyone to help themselves.

Turn the page for a preview...

Leftovers

Great the next day: heat it up and toss it through some noodles.

Chinese Pot Roast Chook

Pot-roasting is easy and I mean really easy. To my mind it is also the simplest way to feed lots of people with minimum mess. In everything goes then you leave it to cook. Season the chicken from the inside – it steams and roasts at the same time so the five-spice and ginger in the middle permeate the soft sweet meat. The vegetables are added to the cooked chook at the last minute so they look fresh and vibrant. Have fun.

Feeds 6

1 large chicken, about 1.5kg

1 thumb-sized piece of fresh root ginger, peeled and chopped

2 spring onions, chopped

1 teaspoon salt

1 teaspoon sugar

1 teaspoon Chinese five-spice powder

2 star anise

1 cinnamon stick

100ml soy sauce

50ml maple syrup

For the vegetables

100g sugar-snap peas

100g mangetout

50g frozen soya beans

100g broccoli

2 spring onions, sliced

1 teaspoon sesame seeds

To serve

1 red chilli, chopped

a handful of chopped coriander

To stuff and roast the chicken

Wash the inside of the chicken well. Mix together the ginger, spring onions, salt, sugar, five-spice powder, star anise and cinnamon.

Fill the chicken with the spice mix and then use a skewer to seal the ends so the filling won't fall out. Shake the chicken then place the bird breast-side up in a large casserole.

Bring the soy sauce and maple syrup to the boil then pour over the chicken.

Put the casserole in the oven, covered with a lid, and cook for 1 hour, then take the lid off, turn the chicken over and continue to cook for another 20 minutes.

To cook the veg

Drop all the vegetables into boiling water and bring back to the boil. Drain and sprinkle with the sesame seeds.

Finally

Carefully drain the excess fat from the chicken pot. Break up the chicken by pulling the pieces apart, being careful not to let the filling fall out, and throw away the carcase.

Toss the vegetables in the liquid in the chicken pot and serve alongside the chicken with some chopped chilli and coriander sprinkled over the veg.

Yoghurt Chicken with Feta and Asparagus

Half Greek barbecue, half Indian tandoori, my grilled, or barbecued, chicken is slathered with loads of lemon and salt and lashings of yoghurt. The Greek influence is all about the feta; the Indian is all about the yoghurt and the barbecue, and the asparagus brings freshness and a bit of colour. It's just as delicious with cucumber, in flatbreads if you like, or just as a salad. Do have it with big glasses of super-cold white wine.

Enough for 6

4 chicken breasts, skin on, sliced in half

6 boned chicken thighs, skin on

2 teaspoons salt

juice of 1 lemon

3 sprigs of thyme

500ml Greek yoghurt

60ml vegetable oil

500g asparagus

100g butter, softened

a handful of freshly chopped mint

1 x 200g block feta cheese

salt and freshly ground black pepper

flatbreads (bought or see page 199 to make your own), to serve (optional)

Puncture the chicken skin with a sharp knife about 6 or 7 times on each piece. Put the whole lot into a big mixing bowl. Sprinkle with the salt, lemon juice and thyme and rub into the chicken with your hands. Add the yoghurt and mix it all again.

Heat the oven to 220°C/gas 7.

Heat a griddle pan. When the pan is really hot, douse the chicken with the vegetable oil, then place as many pieces as possible in the pan (you'll need to do it in batches) and cook for a few minutes or until it is well coloured. Turn the chicken over, adding a little more oil if necessary, and cook for another few minutes. Turn it once more, so it's coloured all over. Put the browned chicken into a roasting tin while you seal the remainder. When it's all sealed, plaster the chicken with any yoghurt still in the bowl. Bake in the oven for 10 minutes then slice a piece off to make sure it's cooked all the way through.

Cook the asparagus by bringing a pot of water to the boil with a little salt, drop the spears in and cook for 4–5 minutes. Drain well and place in a large bowl, stir in the butter and season well.

Lay the buttered asparagus and cooked chicken on a big serving plate, sprinkle over the mint and crumble over the feta. Serve with flatbreads, if you like.

Nanna's Roast Chicken

When I was 5 years old, my nanna showed me how to make the gravy for her amazing roast chicken. It was my first cooking lesson. I had many more over the four years my brothers and I lived with her, stood on a stool beside her, over a combustion stove, listening and learning. Her food was always honest and delicious and generous and has, I believe, made me the cook I am today. I can still smell and taste everything she cooked and as I got better and after much practice she finally entrusted me to cook the roast – this roast, with her gravy. So I dedicate this to you, Nanna. Thank you.

Enough for a family of 6

1 large chicken, about 1.5kg

50g butter, softened

For the stuffing

50g butter

1 onion, diced

100g smoked streaky bacon, roughly chopped

a handful of flat-leaf parsley, roughly chopped

150g fresh breadcrumbs

grated zest of ½ orange

1 Granny Smith apple, peeled and grated

100g sausage meat

salt and freshly ground black pepper

For the mash

2kg potatoes, peeled and cut into chunks about the size of a golf ball

200ml milk, plus extra if necessary

50ml double cream

70g butter, plus extra if necessary

white pepper

For the gravy

2 tablespoons plain flour

To make the stuffing

Heat the oven to 200°C/gas 6.

Melt the butter in a frying pan over a high heat, add a pinch of salt, two grinds of pepper, the onion and bacon and fry for a couple of minutes so the bacon smells good but isn't crispy. Take off the heat and mix in the rest of the ingredients.

To stuff and cook the chicken

Rub the chicken all over with the butter. Stuff both ends of the chicken with the stuffing and tie the chicken legs together with string. Lift the chicken breast-side up into a roasting tin.

Put the chicken in the oven, turn the oven down to 190°C/gas 5 and roast for 1 hour. Turn the chicken over so that it sits on its breast and cook for another 15 minutes.

Remove from the oven, drape the chicken with a sheet of kitchen foil and leave to rest for 20 minutes.

To make the mash

Put the spuds into a large pan, cover with cold water and add 2 teaspoons of salt. Bring to the boil and simmer for about 20 minutes, until tender. Drain well, shaking off all the excess water, then put them back in the pan (off the heat), cover with a tea towel and leave for 5 minutes.

Mash the potatoes with a fork – a fork doesn't squash the spuds like a masher does. Put the pan on a low heat, add the milk, cream and butter and mix well. Add salt and white pepper – lots if you're me.

Almost there...

Nanna's Roast Chicken

...from the previous page

To make the gravy

Take the chicken out of the tin and put it on a board (get rid of the foil). Place the tin over a medium heat and sprinkle the flour over the chicken juices. Use a wooden spoon to scrape the bottom of the tin to lift up all the brown bits and make a paste. Stir and cook for 2–3 minutes. Pour in 250ml of water, turn the heat up, bring to the boil and whisk to get rid of any lumps. Add more water and keep it boiling until it's the consistency you like.

Finally

Pull the chicken apart and pull out the stuffing. Big dish of chicken, big bowl of mash and stacks of gravy. Loads of food for the family.

To mix up the mash

Add the chopped whites of a few spring onions at the same time as the milk and cream and stir through the greens at the end for champ.

Boil the spuds with a chopped onion for potato and onion mash.

My, My Chicken Pie

Pies are my guilty pleasure. It's the pastry – the thick pastry, not cooked until perfectly crisp all the way through, no no no, but with ripples and dimples of what I call 'sog'. I like to make shallow pies with almost equal amounts of pastry and filling. Pie, soggy bits and tomato sauce. Yes, please.

Feeds a family of 8

1 large chicken, about 1.5kg

2 bay leaves

1 large onion, chopped

1 garlic clove, chopped

1 chicken stock cube

1 litre milk, plus extra for brushing

2 leeks, diced

300g button mushrooms

50g butter

50ml water

50g plain flour, plus extra for dusting

200ml double cream

a handful of flat-leaf parsley, chopped

500g all-butter puff pastry (I like the blocks you can roll out)

salt and freshly ground black pepper

The filling

Heat the oven to 200°C/gas 6.

Drop the chicken into a really large pan with the bay leaves, onion, garlic and stock cube and season. Add 500ml of the milk and then top up with water to cover the chicken. Bring to the boil and then slowly simmer for 30 minutes.

Remove the chicken and leave to cool breast-side down on a plate. Strain the cooking liquid, keeping back 500ml. Throw away the rest.

Meanwhile, in a large sauté pan, cook the leeks and mushrooms in the butter over a medium heat with the water until soft. Add the flour and stir to make a paste (a roux), then slowly add the remaining 500ml of milk and the reserved cooking liquid, stirring all the time to make the sauce. Bring to the boil and the sauce will thicken to a sticky, custardy consistency, then stir in the cream.

Peel the skin off the chicken and throw it away (it's not nice in a pie). Strip the chicken carcase of all its meat and tear into thumb-sized pieces.

The pie

Drop the chicken into the leek and mushroom sauce, add the parsley, season and stir it all together. Spoon the pie filling into a lasagne dish and leave the mixture to cool a little.

On a lightly floured worktop, roll out the pastry until it's the size of the top of the dish. Lift up the pastry using the rolling pin and cover the dish. Brush with milk and stab the middle of the pie a few times to make holes to let the air out.

Put the pie on a baking sheet and into the oven it goes. Cook for 30–35 minutes until golden and bubbling around the edges.

A pie must be served with tomato sauce and be careful, the pie will be really hot.

Korean Fried Chicken with Quick Kimchi

One day, a few years ago, I had this yearning for KFC (Korean Fried Chicken) and so I set about trialling and cooking. After much work (and many a friend stuffed full of Korean Fried Chicken), I thought the recipe was perfect. As I typed the final line of the method, my computer crashed. This is my post-Torode meltdown version. Enjoy. And please, when you eat it, use your fingers.

Feeds 4 fried-chicken fans

12 chicken pieces, skin on, bone in

1.5 litres vegetable oil, for frying

For the quick kimchi

1 long Chinese cabbage, cored and cut into quarters

100g gochujang (Korean chilli paste) or half chilli bean paste, half tomato sauce

50ml white vinegar

salt

For the first coating

500g plain flour

3 teaspoons salt

2 teaspoons ground white pepper

1 tablespoon paprika (hot or mild)

1 tablespoon celery salt

1 tablespoon caster sugar

For the second coating

1 x 284ml carton buttermilk

1 x 400g tin cream of chicken soup

For the sticky sauce

2 garlic cloves, chopped

1 thumb-sized piece of fresh root ginger, peeled and grated

2 teaspoons vegetable oil

75g gochujang (Korean chilli paste) or half chilli bean paste, half tomato sauce

50ml rice vinegar

2 teaspoons sesame oil

50ml light soy sauce

2 tablespoons soft light brown sugar

To finish

20g sesame seeds, for sprinkling

Korean Fried Chicken with Quick Kimchi

For the kimchi

Bring a large pan of water to the boil with a little salt. Drop in the cabbage then drain immediately. Mix together the gochujang and vinegar and slather over each clump of cabbage. While still warm, tightly wrap the whole lot in cling film and put a plate on top to weigh it down. Leave for at least 20 minutes before eating but it will keep for a couple of weeks in the fridge.

For the first chicken coating

Take each piece of chicken and slash it once all the way to the bone. This will help the chicken to cook through properly. Run the chicken under cold water and pat dry with kitchen paper.

To make the coating, put all the ingredients in a plastic bag, seal the bag and shake well.

Place the chicken, three or four pieces at a time, in the bag of coating and toss. Arrange the pieces in a roasting tin and continue until all the chicken is coated. Leave in the fridge, uncovered, for 20 minutes.

For the second chicken coating

Mix the buttermilk and soup. Set a wire rack over a tray to stand the chicken on while you coat it.

Roll the coated chicken pieces in the soup mixture, then put them back into the bag of coating and toss. Lay the chicken on the wire rack and continue until all the pieces have been dipped and coated. Leave for 5 minutes, then repeat the dipping and coating process and leave to stand for a further 5 minutes.

To fry and finish the chicken

Heat the oven to 180°C/gas 4.

Pour the vegetable oil into a wok (or use a deep fat fryer) and heat to 180°C. To test if the oil is hot enough, drop one small piece of chicken into it: it should sizzle immediately.

Fry the chicken in batches, four or five pieces at a time, for about 6–8 minutes, or until golden and crusty. Lift out of the fryer, drain on some crumpled kitchen paper then put into a roasting tin. Make sure you return the oil to the correct temperature between each batch.

When it's all been fried, put the tin of chicken in the oven and bake for 10 minutes or until cooked through.

For the sticky sauce

Put the garlic, ginger and oil in a small pan and gently fry over a medium heat for 2 minutes to soften a little – do not allow to colour. Now add the remaining ingredients and bring to the boil. Cook for 2 minutes or until the sauce thickens.

Pour the sauce over the chicken, shaking the tin so that each piece is well coated in the sauce, and then sprinkle with the sesame seeds.

They're on the next page...

Roast Chicken with Crème Fraîche, New Potatoes and Watercress

My love of roast chicken is well documented. It's such a clever, versatile and crowd-pleasing thing. Moist, sweet, salty and delicious, there are few things that deliver as much joy. This is a one-pot wonder. Into the oven it goes, leaving you free to do all those early evening chores: help with the homework, bath the children, clean up the play room, sort out the dog etc., before dinner and that vat of wine.

Feeds 6

1 large chicken, about 1.5kg

200g crème fraîche

½ lemon

4 teaspoons vegetable oil

500g new potatoes

100g watercress

salt and freshly ground black pepper

Heat the oven to 200°C/gas 6.

Season the inside of the chicken with salt and pepper, then spoon the crème fraîche into the cavity. Plug the end of the chicken with the lemon half. Rub the chicken with some of the oil, season well and then place in a roasting tin, breast up.

Roll the potatoes in the remaining oil and then scatter around the chicken.

Place the chicken in the oven and roast for 1 hour 10 minutes without opening the oven door. Leave it.

Pick the largest stems off the watercress and put the lot into a large bowl filled with cold water. Push the watercress under the water and place the bowl in the fridge. The clean watercress will float to the top while all the dirt will sink to the bottom.

Take the chicken out of the oven. Pour the crème fraîche out of the chicken over the potatoes in the tin, then turn the chicken upside down onto a board and leave it to sit for 10 minutes so that all the juices flow back into the breast. It will be done.

Meanwhile, place the tin over a medium heat and bring to the boil, stirring the potatoes around the tin so all the lovely sticky bits come off the sides of the tin and make the sauce. Take it off the heat.

Lift the watercress out of the bowl and shake off the excess water. Put the chicken and potatoes onto a large platter, scatter over the watercress and pour yourself a congratulatory vat of wine.

Try

Mix in root vegetables like turnips and parsnips.

Add a spoonful of mustard for a bit of spice in the crème fraîche.

Duck with Potatoes

This was inspired by a visit to a pretty little bistro in Paris called Allard. Everyone who walks through the door is faced with the open kitchen – for me, a visual feast. If you go, take the time to watch the chefs at work and, like me, marvel at the speed at which they work, the roar of the ovens and all the ducks and huge tins of olives. As a nod to the restaurant and its greatness, here is my version of their dish, with a few potatoes as an added extra.

Should serve 4*

1 duck, about 2kg

1 tablespoon plain flour

200g large pitted black and green olives (nice ones)

10ml red wine vinegar

50ml olive oil

50g butter

6 banana shallots, peeled

300g boiled new potatoes

a large handful of freshly chopped parsley

salt and freshly ground black pepper

* but I like it for 2!

Heat the oven to 170°C/gas 3.

Boil a kettle full of water. Place the duck in the sink and pour over the boiling water – this washes the wax off the duck so it can brown.

Rub the duck all over with flour and salt and pepper. Fill the cavity with half the olives and pour in the vinegar. Skewer the sides of the cavity to stop the olives falling out.

Heat a large ovenproof frying dish over a high heat, add the oil and duck and brown the duck, turning it every minute or so, for 5 minutes. Now add the butter, shallots, potatoes and remaining olives, and give the dish a good shake. Put the dish in the oven and cook for 25 minutes, giving it a good shuffle every so often.

Turn the oven up to 200°C/gas 6, turn the duck over and cook for a further 25–30 minutes.

Take the dish out of the oven, open the cavity of the duck and pour the filling into the dish. Stir well and leave the duck to rest on its breast in the dish for 20 minutes.

Stir the parsley into the potatoes and olives. Carve up the duck and dig in.

Roast Lamb with Rosemary Potatoes

Classic boulangère potatoes with loads of rosemary and the juices of the lamb dripping into them as the meat roasts... this is decadent and delicious but also simple. Laying vegetables around and under meat as it roasts is one of the best ways of getting as much out of it. Put the whole lot in the oven and leave it – what could be easier?

Feeds 8–10

butter, for greasing

2kg large potatoes, peeled and thinly sliced

300g white onions, thinly sliced

200ml strong chicken stock

1 large leg of lamb, with bone, about 2.5kg

loads of rosemary (about 10 large sprigs or branches)

salt and freshly ground black pepper

mint sauce, to serve

Heat the oven to 180°C/gas 4. Butter a large roasting tin generously.

Mix the sliced potatoes and onions with a good amount of salt and pepper and then add the stock. Pour the whole lot into the tin and pat it all down.

Score the leg of lamb deeply and rub well with salt and half the rosemary.

Sit a wire rack on top of the roasting tin. Cover the rack with the remaining rosemary and lay the lamb on top. Put the whole thing in the oven and roast for 1 hour, then turn the tray around and roast for a further 45 minutes, until the lamb is crispy and golden and the potatoes are bubbling underneath.

Take the meat and potatoes out of the oven, discard the rosemary, cover with kitchen foil and leave to rest for 30 minutes before serving with lashings of mint sauce.

Crumbed Lamb Cutlets

This recipe is dedicated to my father, a man who taught me many a thing and has always given me sage advice. He is also the master of these little boned bits of brilliance; they are easy, delicious and quick. Eat them for lunch, dinner, brunch or as a snack, or even cold for breakfast the next day. Thanks Dad x.

Would feed my dad*

200g fresh or dried breadcrumbs

3 eggs, beaten

100g plain flour

12 lamb cutlets

150ml vegetable oil, for frying

salt and freshly ground black pepper

* and me and my two brothers!

Place the breadcrumbs, beaten eggs and flour in separate shallow bowls and season each one.

Dip and coat each cutlet in the flour, repeat the process with the eggs, and then again with the breadcrumbs, making sure the cutlets are well coated at each stage. Wipe the bones clean, lay the cutlets in a tray and chill in the fridge for 30 minutes.

Heat half the oil in a large frying pan, add six of the cutlets, so you don't overcrowd the pan, and fry for about 3–4 minutes on each side on a medium–high heat, until golden. Drain on kitchen paper and keep warm in a low oven while you cook the rest.

These belong with...

Mashed potatoes, chips, Boulangère potatoes (see opposite), neeps and tatties, a big bowl of salad or dipped in tomato sauce.

My Open-top Scallop Dumplings

Scallop dumplings, you say. Well yes, and I have to tell you they are really simple. Think of them as savoury cupcakes: the wrappers are the cups that hold the filling and the scallop slices are the icing. Take a trip to an Asian supermarket, grab some dumpling wrappers and a few bamboo steamer baskets – they are really cheap and will be indispensible. Make loads of dumplings and stack them high because they will disappear as fast as you can make them.

Makes 24

24 round dumpling wrappers

6 small scallops, each sliced into 4 thick rounds

vegetable oil, for greasing

For the filling

100g chicken breast, very, very finely chopped

100g minced pork

1 thumb-sized piece of fresh root ginger, peeled and finely grated

2 spring onions, finely diced

1 small Serrano chilli, diced

1 teaspoon light soy sauce

½ teaspoon sesame oil

Mix all the filling ingredients together and keep them cool.

Place a dumpling wrapper in the palm of your hand or over your fingers, add a good teaspoon of the filling mix and cup your hand or fingers to scrunch the sides up so the wrapper looks like an open sack – the edges will be crimped like a cupcake case. Place a scallop slice on top of the filling. Keep going until you've made all the dumplings. Some may look a bit shabby but that's the point of making your own dumplings.

Oil the base of a steamer basket or baskets. Fill the basket(s) with as many dumplings as can fit comfortably, making sure they are not touching. Put a tight-fitting lid on top of the steamer and place the basket(s) over boiling water – don't let the water touch the baskets. Steam the dumplings for 5 minutes. If you've got two layers, swap the layers after 5 minutes and cook for 2 minutes more. Cook and serve in batches.

Dip...

Serve the dumplings with a few different dipping sauces, such as mirin, soy mixed with sliced ginger, sweet chilli or XO sauce.

Thai Red Pork Curry with Beansprouts

A curry is not a curry is not a curry: every curry is different and the translation of the word is simply 'gravy'. The most important part of any curry is the gravy – the sauce. There should be lots of it; the meat is just a flavouring as are all the tasty bits floating around it and that is because a good curry should be served with lots and lots of rice. My red curry paste is for the enthusiast, and a good-quality paste in a plastic tub is fine. You can buy the tubs in most supermarkets and you only need 2 tablespoons of the paste for this dish. (Few Thais actually make their own paste!)

Feeds 6–8

For my red curry paste

20 long dried red chillies

1 teaspoon coriander seeds

1 teaspoon cumin seeds

1 small piece of fresh mace

5 white peppercorns

2 tablespoons dried shrimp paste (belacan)

50g garlic, sliced

50g Thai or banana shallots, sliced

50g coriander roots (stalks at a push), cleaned

100g galangal, peeled and chopped

3 lemongrass stalks, outer leaves removed and inner stalks chopped

pinch of salt

7 frozen lime leaves, cut into thin strips

If you're making my curry paste...

Snap the stalks off the dried red chillies, shake out the seeds and throw them away, then soak the chillies in a bowl of hot water for 30 minutes until they plump up. Strain. Now wash your hands in cold water!

Put all the spices in a dry pan over a high heat and roast for about 2 minutes until they colour. Grind them to a powder using a mortar and pestle or a spice grinder.

Wrap the shrimp paste in foil and roast in the dry frying pan for 4 minutes until fragrant.

Put the garlic and shallots in a food processor or pound using a pestle and mortar. Add the coriander roots, soaked chillies, galangal, lemongrass and salt and whizz or pound until a paste begins to form. Then add the roasted shrimp paste, the spices and the lime leaves. Blend to a smooth paste. Freeze any leftover paste in ice cube trays.

Thai Red Pork Curry with Beansprouts

For the curry

2 x 400g tins coconut milk

2 tablespoons Thai red curry paste (if you're not making your own)

1 tablespoon palm sugar (or at a push use soft brown sugar)

500g fatty boneless pork shoulder, large cubes, fat on

a small handful of Kaffir lime leaves

1 tablespoon fish sauce

a handful of Thai basil leaves

a handful of coriander, leaves picked

100g beansprouts

Curry time

Open the tins of coconut milk, make a hole in the top of the thick coconut milk, strain any thin coconut milk into a bowl and keep to one side.

Spoon the thick coconut milk from the tins into a wok or large saucepan and melt it gently over a low heat. Add 2 tablespoons of the curry paste and increase the heat a little so it starts to sizzle. Now add the palm sugar and cook for a few minutes until the paste starts to colour – the paste will slowly become more of a jam: rich and dark red and fragrant; this will take about 5 minutes.

Add the pork, stir the whole lot around until it is coated in the jam. Cook for about 5 minutes, then add the reserved thin coconut milk from the bowl, lime leaves and fish sauce. Now take 1 of the coconut milk tins, fill it with warm water and pour the water into the pan.

Let the sauce bubble for about 15 minutes, until the oil in the coconut milk starts to come to the surface, then reduce the heat to a simmer and cook for another 15 minutes until the meat is tender.

Mix the herbs and beansprouts and scatter them over the curry. Place the pot in the middle of the table and serve with loads of rice.

Shake it up...

Lots of things can be added to the curry as it cooks: butternut squash at the beginning; aubergines in the middle; raw prawns for the last 5 minutes; raw scallops at the last minute; or tofu as you serve.

Posh Curry Cutlets *

There won't be any leftovers when you serve this clever, easy-to-cook dish to your friends. Once cooked, the curried racks of lamb can either be sliced into cutlets or served whole as a grand centrepiece. Should you not have the time to make the Madras paste from scratch, that's fine, you can use a good-quality jar of paste instead. Sometimes it's okay to cheat.

*Turn the page for the butch version

Feeds 6–8

2 x 8-bone racks of lamb, trimmed

24 Charlotte potatoes, peeled

1 x 400g tin chickpeas, drained

200ml thick Greek yoghurt

small bunch of coriander, chopped

For the Madras paste

1 teaspoon ground cardamom

2 teaspoons ground cinnamon

2 teaspoons fenugreek seeds

1 teaspoon black peppercorns

2 teaspoons garam masala

4 teaspoons coriander seeds

1 teaspoon ground turmeric

1 teaspoon fennel seeds

2 teaspoons mustard seeds

2 teaspoons dried chilli powder

1 onion, chopped

6 garlic cloves

80g fresh root ginger, peeled

50g butter

50ml vegetable oil

150ml brown malt vinegar

The paste

Put all the spices in a dry pan over a high heat and toast for about 2 minutes until they colour and become fragrant. Grind them to a powder using a mortar and pestle or a spice grinder (a food processor doesn't do the job).

Using a mortar and pestle or food-processor, purée the onion, garlic and ginger.

Place a large, heavy-based frying pan over a medium heat add the butter, oil and the purée and cook for 2 minutes. Add the ground spices and vinegar and mix to a paste. Bring to the boil, then reduce the heat and simmer for 5 minutes, until bubbling, fragrant and the paste starts to split.

The lamb

Heat the oven to 200°C/gas 6.

Score the fat on the racks of lamb deeply. Place the racks, fat-side down, in a cold frying pan. Turn the heat up to medium and leave for a good 5 minutes, until the fat renders and your kitchen smells of roast lamb.

Meanwhile, par-cook the potatoes in a large pan of boiling water for just 10 minutes. Drain and transfer the potatoes to a roasting tin. Add the chickpeas and a tablespoon of the curry paste and mix well. Spread the mixture evenly over the roasting tin.

Rub the remaining curry paste all over the lamb and then put the racks of lamb fat-side up on top of the potatoes. Cook in the oven for 25 minutes (do not open the oven door). Yes, 25 minutes.

Remove from the oven and leave the lamb to rest for 10 minutes. Mix the potatoes and chickpeas with the yoghurt and coriander, then tuck in.

And to posh it up even more...

Serve the cutlets with grilled tomatoes, some dressed watercress or a tasty green salad.

Sloppy Joe Bolognese

Melted cheese and mince on toast, yep that's right. You can do whatever you want with this sauce (make a pie or serve it with spaghetti), but I like to serve it on toast with lashing of butter, either hot or cold. Bolognese sauce is one of those things that you should always have in your fridge or freezer.

Makes 8*

2 onions

2 large carrots, peeled and finely chopped

2 celery sticks, finely chopped

1 leek, finely chopped

2 garlic cloves

1 sprig of rosemary, leaves picked

1 teaspoon dried oregano or thyme

50ml vegetable oil

1kg minced beef (not too fine or fatty)

50g plain flour

500ml beef stock

1 x 400g tin chopped tomatoes

250ml red wine

2 bay leaves

Worcestershire sauce

salt and freshly ground black pepper

To serve

8 slices of white bread

butter, for spreading

200g Cheddar cheese, grated

* with sauce leftover to freeze

Put the veg and herbs in a food processor and blend until it forms a rough paste.

Put the oil and the veggie paste in a large heavy-based pan and cook over a medium heat for about 5 minutes, until the smell of the raw onion has gone. Add a good amount of salt and pepper and cook for another few minutes. Add the mince, turn the heat up and cook it over a high heat for about 10 minutes or until the mince has some colour.

Sprinkle the flour over the meat, stir and cook for a couple of minutes – the flour needs to cook a bit or it tastes a bit gloggy. Slowly pour in the stock, tomatoes and red wine, add the bay leaves and simmer for 1 hour, stirring every so often, until the stock has reduced and the sauce has become thick. Remove the pan from the heat and add a good glug of Worcestershire sauce.

Heat the grill to high. Place the bread on a baking sheet, toast it on one side, turn it over and butter it, then spoon a good amount of the Bolognese onto each slice, sprinkle over the cheese and place under the grill until the cheese has melted and bubbles. Serve with lashings of tomato sauce.

Beef Rendang

Rendang, rendang, rendang. You need to know one of the John Torode favourites. As I write this I am thinking I must make it this weekend and freeze some because it freezes so well. It's a fail-safe – a go-to. When I pass a butcher and spy a big hunk of beef shin it seems to set my brain to default mode: beef rendang time. Rendang is very rich so eat a little but often. Small portions, with rice, roti, cucumber salad and a relish or two, will make for a feast. Oh and remember to freeze the rest.

Feeds 8

40g coriander seeds

1 teaspoon cumin seeds

1 teaspoon ground turmeric

2 lemongrass stalks, bashed

50ml vegetable oil

3 large onions, finely chopped

6 garlic cloves, grated

6 red chillies, de-seeded and chopped

2 thumb-sized pieces of fresh root ginger, peeled and minced

1.5kg stewing beef (I think shin is the very best), cut into pieces about 2.5cm square

2 bay leaves

2 x 400g tins coconut milk

1 x 100g block creamed coconut

500ml hot strong veal or beef stock

Put the coriander and cumin seeds and the turmeric into a dry frying pan and roast over a high heat for 2 minutes. Grind to a powder using a mortar and pestle, then add the lemongrass and pound until it forms a paste and is as smooth as possible.

In a wok or large pan, heat the vegetable oil. Drop in the onions, garlic, chillies, ginger and the spice paste and cook gently until the onions are softened and your kitchen starts to smell like Asia. Add the meat and bay leaves, increase the heat to high and stir to coat completely in the spices and flavourings. Cook for a few minutes until the meat has coloured a little.

Add the coconut milk and creamed coconut, bring to the boil, then add the hot stock. Turn the heat to medium. Stir often, scraping the bottom of the wok with a wooden spoon so the paste doesn't stick. Over the next hour the liquid will simmer and reduce to become a thick sauce. It will need to be stirred constantly for the last 5–10 minutes or so, so that it doesn't stick.

This is a dry curry: all the sweet coconut and spices should end up wrapped around the tender chunks of meat and there should be very little sauce. Keep cooking it if it's not thick enough.

Turn the page for a rendang in pictures...

Don't forget the...

Rice, roti, cucumber salad and lots of fresh herbs.

Not quite...

...just right!

Roast Rib of Beef with...

Roast beef, Sundays and Sunday best are words that I feel belong together and evoke many a childhood memory. However, it was much later in life that I discovered the majesty of the Yorkshire pudding as being Australian it was not something I grew up with. Thankfully that has all changed and I have seen the light. Beef and Yorkshire pudding go together like love and marriage. Great roast beef has crispy bits, fatty bits, soggy bits and all the other bits that make up a proper roast.

Feeds 10–12 hungry people

1 x 5-bone rib of beef, about 5kg, trimmed by the butcher

vegetable oil, for greasing

4 carrots, peeled and cut in half lengthways

salt and freshly ground black pepper

For the crust

1 large onion, diced

80g butter

300g fresh white breadcrumbs

2 eggs, beaten

200g Dijon mustard

200ml water

First thing in the morning, remove the beef from the fridge to allow it to come to room temperature. Stab the fat really well all over (but don't cut the string holding it together).

Heat the oven to 200°C/gas 6.

Rub the beef all over with a little oil and lots of salt and pepper, then make the crust. Fry the onions in the butter over a medium heat, until soft, then stir in the breadcrumbs and take off the stove.

Whisk the eggs, mustard and water together, then add the wet mix to the breadcrumbs and stir until you have a stuffing consistency.

Spread the crust evenly over the beef, leaving the ends free of covering. Cover the crust only with well-greased kitchen foil.

Place the carrots in a large roasting tin and sit the beef on them – the carrots will act as a trivet and let the heat circulate around the rather large hunk of meat. Roast in the oven for 2½ hours.

Remove the foil from the beef crust and cook for a further 30 minutes. Take the beef out of the oven (leave the oven on if you're making the Yorkshire puds) and leave to rest for a good 30 minutes – giving you the time you need to cook the Yorkshires.

Yorkshire Puddings

This recipe makes a lot of Yorkshire puddings. Remember that I'm an Aussie and I didn't grow up with the Yorkie phenomenon so I'm making up for lost time. It took me a good couple of years of searching, testing and failing before I got the recipe right but I think this is it; these puds are pretty special.

Makes 24

80ml melted beef dripping or vegetable oil

8 eggs, at room temperature

½ teaspoon salt

500g plain flour

600ml milk

You will need 2 muffin tins or Yorkshire pudding tins

Divide the beef dripping between the muffin tins and put them into the oven. Beat the eggs with the salt. Sift the flour twice to aerate it. Add the milk to the eggs and beat, then add the flour and beat well until there are no lumps. Pour the batter into a jug.

Take the tins out of the oven and fill each hole until it's half full – be careful as the fat will be very hot. Put the tins back in the oven and cook for 20 minutes, until risen and golden. Yum.

Roast beef and Yorkshires... it's heaven!

Don't forget...

The Yorkshire puddings can be frozen once cooked and cooled. If you've got a busy day, make the batter in advance, chill it and then cook as above. Clever.

We are all busy so these recipes are for times you need to cook fast. You might have to shop for ingredients in advance but once you have the necessary: bingo – food on the table.

in a rush

Purple Sprouting Broccoli, Linguine, Chilli and Pine Nuts

This is one of my quick, quick, the kids are starving (so am I) recipes. The amount of chilli you use is up to you; I serve some on the side for those who like it. Chopped sausages are a good addition: push the sausages out of their skins and cook them with the chilli and onions for a more blokey type of feast.

For 4–6

50ml olive oil, plus extra for the pasta water

500g linguine

1 red onion, sliced

4 garlic cloves, sliced

2 long red chillies, split in half, de-seeded and sliced (optional)

300g purple sprouting broccoli, boiled for 2 minutes

20g pine nuts

salt and freshly ground black pepper

a big hunk of Parmesan, to serve

Bring a really large pan of water (about 5 litres) to the boil with 2 teaspoons of olive oil and add the pasta. Cook the pasta according to the packet instructions.

Meanwhile, heat the remaining oil in a frying pan over a low–medium heat. Add the onion and garlic, cook gently and slowly for a few minutes until they are soft; keep the temperature low. Season the onions well with loads of salt and pepper. Drop in the chilli (if using), and cook for a minute or so. Now drop in the cooked broccoli, give it a good stir and cook for a couple of minutes so that the broccoli gets hot. Add the pine nuts.

Drain the pasta and pour it into the pan with the onion and broccoli.

Turn up the heat and toss everything together.

Spoon onto plates or pile into a large heated bowl, and make sure there is loads of Parmesan to grate over the top.

Or try...

For grown-ups you can add a few anchovies.

Use different varieties of broccoli or Romanesco cauliflower, or even add some bitter leaves, like radicchio.

Asparagus with Black Butter and Capers

Asparagus is one of my top five things. I properly adore it. The asparagus season in the UK is from some time in April to Father's Day and I believe that is when, and only when, it should be eaten. Keep it simple when it comes to cooking asparagus. It's lovely simply buttered or served with hollandaise sauce. This version is super delicious too.

Serves 6–8 as a side

2 large bunches of fresh asparagus

100g butter, softened

50g capers

1 lemon, cut in half

a handful of freshly chopped flat-leaf parsley

salt and freshly ground black pepper

Prep the asparagus

The spears have a tough base and a tender stem and tip and they will naturally snap towards the base where the white starts to turn to green. Break each spear and discard the bases.

Cook it

Fill a large pan with water and some salt and bring to the boil. Tie the asparagus in bundles of 12 using twine or cooking string, then drop the bundles into the boiling water. Return to the boil and cook for 4 minutes – don't cook for any longer or the asparagus will be sloppy and have no texture and the tips will disintegrate. Take out of the water and cut the twine.

Make the sauce

Place the butter in a large frying pan over a medium heat. When the butter is really hot it will scoot around the pan and start to burn. As soon as that happens, drop in the asparagus, add the capers, and sizzle on as high a heat as possible until the butter coats the asparagus. Squeeze over half the lemon, throw over the parsley and serve with wedges of the remaining lemon half.

Spaghetti with Prawns and Macadamia Nuts

Sweet prawns and salty macadamia nuts are an interesting combo – I reckon it's a good one. Just add a little chilli and it becomes a prawn satay-cum-noodle thing.

Feeds 4–6

12 large raw prawns with heads and shells

400g spaghetti

50ml vegetable oil

80g butter

1 long red chilli, de-seeded and diced

100ml crème fraîche

a small handful of freshly chopped flat-leaf parsley

salt and freshly ground black pepper

100g macadamia nuts, chopped

Peel the prawns and reserve all the heads and shells. Chop the prawns into small pieces and set aside.

Cook the spaghetti in a large pan of salted boiling water according to the instructions on the packet.

Meanwhile, put the prawn heads and shells in a large frying pan over a high heat and crush them with the back of a spoon. Turn up the heat and let them toast for a good 5 minutes, moving them around once or twice, until they turn pink and start to smell like a barbecued prawn. Once they have some colour, add the oil and let it sizzle, take the pan off the heat and add half the butter – it should sizzle again. Season. You will now have prawn-flavoured butter.

Strain the butter into a large bowl, pressing down on the shells with the back of a spoon to squeeze out all the juice. Throw the shells away.

Pour the prawn-flavoured butter back into the frying pan and add the remaining butter. Turn up the heat, add the chopped prawns and chilli and cook for 2 minutes or until the prawns turn pink – they should smell good.

Drain the spaghetti and drop the wet spaghetti into the frying pan with the prawns. Spoon in the crème fraîche, throw in the parsley and give it all a good mix to coat the pasta with sauce. Top with the macadamia nuts.

Pork Escalopes with Couscous, Harissa and Yoghurt

Moorish food is all the rage. The smells alone are enough to transport you to a far-off place. Here we have sweet pork that's quickly grilled with lots of paprika and served with smoky harissa and spicy couscous. You can make your own harissa if you like (see page 198) or just buy it in a jar. I like to serve the couscous at room temperature but if you'd prefer to serve it hot, simply cover the bowl with cling film and place in the microwave to heat up.

Serves 6

For the couscous

500g couscous

50g butter

100g raisins

400ml boiling water

50ml olive oil

1 teaspoon ground cumin

1 teaspoon smoked paprika

1 long red chilli, de-seeded and diced

½ a handful of freshly chopped coriander

10 mint leaves, chopped

juice of 1 lime

salt and freshly ground black pepper

For the pork

6 large pork escalopes

60ml vegetable oil

1 tablespoon smoked paprika

To serve

harissa (see page 198, or use a shop-bought jar)

100g thick yoghurt

Make the couscous

Put the couscous, butter, raisins and a good pinch of salt into a large bowl, pour over the boiling water, tightly cover the bowl with cling film and leave to stand in a warm place for 10 minutes.

Meanwhile, heat the olive oil in a heavy-based frying pan, add the cumin and paprika, stir and cook over a medium heat for about 2 minutes, until fragrant and the spices change colour. Add the chilli, give it a stir, then take it off the heat.

When the couscous is ready, use a fork to fluff it up, then add the spiced oil, along with the coriander, mint and lime juice and mix well.

Cook the pork

Heat a griddle pan over a high heat. Rub the pork all over with the vegetable oil, smoked paprika and some salt and pepper. When the griddle is smoking hot, lay the escalopes down and cook for about a minute on each side. You want the escalopes to really colour – they should almost char.

Serve with the couscous, harissa and yoghurt.

Japanese Chicken Noodles with Sake

This very quick noodle dish is a crowd-pleaser. I prefer to use pre-cooked thick, wormy udon noodles, which are now available in most supermarkets. Preparation is the key to this dish: everything needs to be sliced and ready for a really fast cook.

Feeds 4–6

50ml vegetable oil

4 boneless chicken breasts, skin on, sliced lengthways into 2cm-thick strips

80g fresh root ginger, peeled and sliced into small slithers

2 garlic cloves, sliced very, very finely

6 spring onions, cut into strips

200ml sake

800g ready-cooked udon noodles

70ml soy sauce

3 eggs, beaten

The first bit is all about the preparation so make sure that everything is cut and ready for a really quick cook.

Heat the oil in a wok or large frying pan over a high heat. Add the chicken, let it sizzle, then add the ginger and garlic and cook for a couple of minutes, then stir until there is a little colour on the chicken but be careful not to burn the ginger. Add the spring onions, followed by the sake and bring to the boil. Immediately drop in the noodles and stir so the noodles get hot – this will take about a minute. Add the soy sauce and cook for another minute, then pour in the eggs, stir and cook for another minute or so until they become a sauce that wraps around everything. Eat hot.

It's almost as quick as turning the page...

Corn Chip Chicken (and Quick Slaw if you want)

This recipe was born out of an adventure. While filming *John Torode's Australia*, I had to feed a load of young surf lifesavers something healthy but appealing so I invented this for the 'nippers' as they are called. The tortilla chips are crushed up to become the coating for strips of chicken. The slaw is an extra if you want. My kids just like it with tomato sauce.

Feeds 6

For the chicken

200ml crème fraîche

1 egg, beaten

4 large skinless and boneless chicken breasts

1 x 200g bag of tortilla chips

100ml vegetable oil

For the quick slaw

4 teaspoons olive oil

½ green cabbage, shredded as finely as possible

freshly ground black pepper

50g Parmesan shavings

Coat the chook

Heat the oven to 160°C/gas 3. Mix together the crème fraîche and egg in a large bowl. Cut the chicken into finger-sized strips, then roll them in the crème fraîche mix.

Crush the tortilla chips into little bits in their bag. Now drop all the coated chicken into the bag, roll the top down and shake the bag around a lot so that each piece of chicken is coated in corn chip crumbs. Pour the chicken out of the bag onto a tray and leave for 5 minutes so the corn chips go a little soggy – they will fry better that way.

Quickly make the slaw

Mix the olive oil, cabbage and pepper in a large bowl. Spread over a large platter and throw over the Parmesan.

Fry the chook

Heat the oil in a large frying pan over a high heat. Place as many pieces of chicken as you can fit in the base of the pan without any of them touching – you will probably have to fry the chicken in batches. Cook for 2 minutes on each side, until brown and crisp. Put the cooked chicken on a baking sheet and keep warm in the oven while you cook the remaining bits.

Serve up a big bowl of the chicken strips – with the slaw, or not.

Or try...

The corn-chip coating works on all manner of meat and fish, such as strips of cod or plaice, or schnitzels or prawns.

One-pot Spicy Rice with Chicken and Prawns

What would a busy home cook do without one-pot wonders? Parents all over the world will understand what it means to have very little time and the joy of having (almost) no washing up. So when I have to do family taxiing stuff I pop this in the oven, race to pick the kids up, and 25 minutes later it's ready when I walk in the door so that the little (or not so little!) ones have food when they get home… And we all know how important that is.

Feeds a hungry family of 6

60ml olive oil

2 onions, diced

2 garlic cloves, crushed

6 boned chicken thighs, each cut into 4 pieces

200g chorizo, sliced

1 teaspoon smoked paprika

1 long red chilli, chopped (optional)

400g good-quality long grain or paella rice

1 x 400g tin chopped tomatoes

100ml white wine

500ml vegetable stock (made up with 2 vegetable stock cubes)

300g large peeled prawns, cleaned

a good handful of coriander leaves

salt and freshly ground black pepper

Heat the oven to 200°C/gas 6.

Put the oil, onion and garlic in a large casserole. Gently cook over a medium heat for a couple of minutes, stirring all the time. Drop in the chicken, chorizo, paprika and chilli, if using, give everything a really good stir and leave for 1 minute over a high heat. Pour in the rice and stir again, then season well with salt and pepper. Add the tomatoes, wine and stock and stir again. Cover with a lid and bring to the boil.

Now put the casserole into the oven for 25 minutes. Remove from the oven, carefully lift off the lid (it will be really hot) and lay the prawns over the top of the spicy rice. Put back in the oven, without the lid, and cook for a further 10 minutes until the top of the rice is a bit crispy.

Sprinkle with coriander, take the casserole to the table and share with your family.

Thai Omelette Stuffed with Pork

An Asian omelette is not what you might expect. It is deep-fried in a wok rather than pan-fried with butter. The oil needs to be really hot, otherwise the egg will soak it up and make the omelette greasy. My version is filled with minced pork and flavoured with the tart and spicy juice of a lime but they are also great filled with crab, minced chicken or vegetables.

For 4

For the filling

2 tablespoons vegetable oil

1 garlic clove, crushed

1 small onion, diced

225g minced pork

2 spring onions, thinly sliced

2 teaspoons fish sauce

125g cherry tomatoes, quartered

2 tablespoons soft light brown sugar

juice of 1 lime

¼ teaspoon ground black pepper

a handful of freshly chopped coriander

For the omelette

300ml vegetable oil

6 large eggs, beaten

1 tablespoon fish sauce

1 teaspoon soft light brown sugar

Make the filling

Heat a wok over a high heat. Add the oil and swirl it around. Add the garlic and fry for 1 minute or until it turns golden. Reduce the heat to medium, add the onion and cook for about 5 minutes, until soft. Add the minced pork, spring onions and fish sauce and toss together. Stir in the tomatoes, sugar and lime juice, bring to a simmer and cook for 5 minutes, or until the sauce thickens. Stir in the pepper and coriander then spoon into a bowl and keep warm.

Make the omelettes

Wipe the wok clean. Heat the oil over a high heat to 180°C. Mix the eggs with the fish sauce and sugar. Pour half the egg mixture into the oil and stir for 30 seconds – a raft of omelette will float to the surface. The raft needs to cook for 3–5 minutes, or until it has colour. Using two large spoons, lift the omelette out of the oil and set it aside to drain on a clean tea towel. Repeat to cook the second half of the egg mixture, putting it onto a second clean tea towel.

Spoon half the filling mixture onto the first omelette and roll it up like a Swiss roll using the tea towel. Repeat with the second one. Cut the omelettes into 5cm slices and serve.

Turn over for a 'how to' in pics...

Seared Salmon with Indian Spiced Lentils

I like my salmon one of two ways: smoked or seared. When I say seared, read charred on the outside and a little rare inside. The dark outside and sweet soft inside is a good combo. Don't let the salmon cook too long or it will be fish-flavoured cotton wool. Make the lentils the day before if you are really short of time; they last for a few days in the fridge.

For 5–6

For the spiced lentils

100g Puy lentils

2 tablespoons vegetable oil

1 garlic clove, grated

25g fresh root ginger, peeled and grated

1 long red chilli, de-seeded and diced

1 medium onion, grated

3 cardamom pods, crushed

1 teaspoon ground coriander

1 teaspoon ground cumin

1 teaspoon ground ginger

2 large ripe plum tomatoes, chopped

300ml vegetable stock

1 tablespoon crème fraîche

a good handful of coriander leaves

50g butter

For the salmon

800g salmon fillet, skin on

2 tablespoons olive oil

salt and freshly ground black pepper

Lentils

Rinse the lentils and put them into a large saucepan. Cover with fresh water and bring to the boil, then cook for 5 minutes. Drain and put the lentils to one side.

Heat the vegetable oil in a saucepan and gently fry the garlic, ginger, chilli and onion over a medium heat, until golden – about 4–5 minutes.

Add the dried spices and cook for a minute or two, until fragrant. Now add the part-cooked lentils and stir well so they are coated in the spicy mixture. Drop in the chopped tomatoes and turn the heat up. Squash the tomatoes with the back of a spoon and when everything in the pan is steaming hot add the stock.

Bring to the boil then turn the heat down to a simmer and bubble gently for 10 minutes. The lentils should now be tender and soft, but if they're not, leave them to cook until they are.

Salmon

Heat the oven to 200°C/gas 6. Heat a griddle or frying pan over a very high heat for a good 10 minutes until scorchio (really hot).

Rub the salmon all over with oil and place it on the griddle lengthways, skin-side up. Be prepared to open all your windows and doors; this is gonna smoke – lots!

After about 4 minutes lift the salmon and give it a quarter turn to the left and cook for a further 4 minutes. Flip it onto a baking sheet, skin-side down and put it in the oven. Roast for 5 minutes. Take it out, turn it back over and peel off the skin (throw the skin away). Pull the salmon apart with two forks – it should naturally flake.

Finish

While the salmon is in the oven, take a third of the lentil mixture and pop it in a food processor with the crème fraîche. Blitz for a minute to make a thick purée – this will thicken the sauce. Pour the purée back into the pan, let it bubble then take it off the heat. Drop in the coriander leaves and butter. Serve the salmon and lentils together on a big platter and let people help themselves.

Baked Cod, Tomatoes, Lemon and Olives

Being an Aussie, I didn't grow up with cod but wow, I think it's ace. It deserves to be cooked in a way that keeps the sweet flesh moist so that it falls apart at the seams and this is a fool-proof traybake fish dish that will guarantee it does just that. All the vegetables are roasted for a good 20 minutes first, then the fish is plonked on top and put in the oven. It is simple as simple can be. I like this with mashed potato but serve it with whatever you want…

Feeds 4

24 cherry or pomodorino tomatoes, halved

2 banana shallots, cut into quarters

150g each of black and green olives

50ml olive oil

4 x 180g hunks of cod, skin on

1 lemon, cut into 4 thick slices

salt and freshly ground black pepper

rock salt, to serve

a handful of flat-leaf parsley, roughly chopped, to serve

Heat the oven to 200°C/gas 6.

In a bowl mix the together the tomatoes, shallots, olives and half the oil and season with salt and pepper. Mix it all together. Pour into a baking tray and slide the tray into the hot oven. Leave the veg to roast for 20 minutes. The toms will soften, the shallots will roast and brown, and the olives will shrivel and become strong and salty. Take the tray out and rest it somewhere safe.

Rub the cod all over with a slice of the lemon, now lay the lemon slices on top of the tomatoes and place a piece of cod, skin-side up, on top of each slice. Rub the remaining oil over the skin. Slide the tray back into the oven for 10 minutes, no more.

Take the tray out, lift the cod gently onto warm dishes, discard the lemon, peel the skin off the fish and throw that away too. Sprinkle the fish with a little rock salt.

Pour the tomato mix into a bowl, and using a fork, sort of squash the tomatoes a little so they become a chunky sauce. Spoon the tomatoes over the fish and scatter over the parsley if you want to be fancy.

Or try...

Once the fish is on the plates, I sometimes mix a good tablespoon of crème fraîche into the tray to make creamed tomatoes.

Scallops with Rocket and Chilli

The River Café is one of my favourite places to eat and has been for two decades. For as long as I can remember, grilled squid with chilli and rocket has been on the menu but when they can't get squid they use scallops – the inspiration for this dish. Simple, fast and delicious, I like it a lot. This recipe is in honour of the great Rose Gray – I miss you.

Serves 4

12 large scallops

50ml vegetable oil

2 tablespoons olive oil

2 long red chillies, de-seeded and diced

juice of ½ lemon

100g rocket

salt and freshly ground black pepper

lemon wedges, to serve

Heat a frying pan over a high heat. Rub each scallop with vegetable oil and season with salt and pepper.

When the pan is hot, and I mean really hot, add the scallops and cook for at least 2 minutes until they are golden brown underneath. Turn, adding a little more oil if the scallops aren't sizzling, and cook until coloured on both sides. Flip again and cook for a further 2 minutes.

While the scallops are cooking, put the olive oil, chillies and lemon juice in a large bowl.

Once cooked, drop the hot scallops into the bowl of chilli and stir to coat.

Divide the rocket between the plates, drop the scallops on top and serve with wedges of lemon and a glass of chilled white wine.

Grilled Squid with Spiced Chickpeas

I love leftovers and this is born from the remains of a curry takeaway. I added leftover chana masala to some squid and it worked a treat. So, if you can't be bothered to make the chickpeas yourself or are really up against it time-wise, pick up some chana masala from the curry house on your way home and this dish will take 5 minutes max. Cool.

Serves 4–6

80ml vegetable oil

30g butter

1 large onion, roughly chopped

4 garlic cloves, crushed

½ teaspoon cayenne pepper

½ teaspoon ground cumin

½ teaspoon ground coriander

½ teaspoon garam masala

½ teaspoon turmeric

¼ teaspoon ground ginger

1 x 400g tin chickpeas (don't drain them)

1 x 200g tin chopped tomatoes

1 lemon

a handful of coriander leaves, finely chopped

400g squid, cleaned and cut into matchbox-sized pieces

salt and freshly ground black pepper

Make the spiced chickpeas

Put a large frying pan over a medium heat, add 20ml of the oil and the butter and cook the onion and garlic for about 2 minutes, until soft. Now add all the spices and 2 teaspoons of salt and cook for 2–3 minutes, stirring all the time, until coloured and the kitchen smells like your local Indian.

Open the chickpea tin and drain half the liquid. Pour the rest of the liquid and all the chickpeas into the pan and bring to the boil. Add the tomatoes and give it a really good stir. Increase the heat, bring to the boil, season and cook for 3 minutes or until you have a sauce. Add a squeeze of lemon juice then the fresh coriander to the chickpea mix and stir well. Check the seasoning. Cover and keep warm.

Cook the squid

Heat a heavy-based frying pan or griddle. Mix the remaining 60ml of oil with the squid and when the pan is very hot, add half the squid and a good grind of pepper and let it fry for 2 minutes – don't move it. Now give it a quick stir, then cook for another minute or so. Remove from the pan, finely slice the squid, then add it to the chickpea mixture.

Cook the second batch of squid in the same way (you won't need to add any oil), slice and mix with the chickpeas. Add another squeeze of lemon and check the seasoning.

Soft-shell Crab

A soft-shell crab recipe in this chapter? Absolutely and it deserves its place as it is so quick and so easy and so tasty. You do need to have all the ingredients and some are a little difficult to find, like the dried mango powder, but with a little planning your store cupboard can become an Aladdin's cave, as can your freezer. Soft-shell crabs are always sold frozen so they're really useful as I can quickly grab a few from the freezer should I want.

Feeds 4

For the quick spiced mayo

1 egg yolk

1 tablespoon Dijon mustard

100ml tarragon vinegar

100ml olive oil

200ml vegetable oil

1 large red chilli, de-seeded and chopped

For the crab

1.5 litres vegetable oil, for frying

12 frozen soft-shell crabs, defrosted

50g plain flour

1 egg, beaten

20ml milk

150g gram flour (chickpea flour)

1 teaspoon paprika

1 teaspoon ground coriander

1 teaspoon dried mango powder (available from Indian grocers)

salt and freshly ground black pepper

Make the mayo

Place all the ingredients in a bowl and use a hand blender to blend until smooth and creamy.

Prep the crabs

Pour the vegetable oil into a wok and heat to 180°C or until it starts to shimmer.

Dip the wet crabs in the plain flour to coat and set to one side.

Mix the egg and the milk with a little salt and pepper in a shallow bowl. In a separate bowl mix together the gram flour, the spices and the mango powder. Now dip the floured crabs in the egg mixture and then roll them in the spice mixture, making sure they are well coated.

Cook the crabs

Drop half the crabs into the hot oil, cook for 2 minutes, turning them over after 1 minute. Drain them on a wire rack while you fry the rest.

Serve the crabs with the spiced mayo.

Or go fancy...

Think mango chutney, lime pickle, some flatbreads, naan or chapatis and cucumber salad.

Do the same with prawns, squid or scallops.

Minute Steaks with Mushrooms and Crispy Fried Eggs

Mushrooms, eggs and steaks are just a great combo and it works as a quick meal for breakfast, lunch or dinner. For this recipe, you will need really large flat mushrooms, they should be the size of saucers – yes, that big! Strangely, they actually take longer to cook than the steak.

Feeds 4

200g large flat mushrooms

100ml olive oil

1 shallot, diced

2 handfuls of chopped flat-leaf parsley

4 eggs

4 minute steaks, weighing about 175g each

salt and freshly ground black pepper

Mushrooms

Place a cast iron griddle pan over a high heat and leave it to get really hot.

Place the mushrooms, open-side up, on the griddle, drizzle with 30ml of the oil and season. Cook for 2 minutes, then turn over and cook for another 2 minutes, until soft, then lift out of the pan.

Put 50ml of the oil in a large frying pan, add the shallot and cook over a medium heat for 2 minutes. Cut the mushrooms into thick slices and add them to the pan. Leave to cook for a couple of minutes without moving either the pan or the mushrooms, until they colour. Turn the mushrooms over and cook for a further 2 minutes so they're coloured all over. Season and add the parsley, transfer to a bowl and keep warm.

Eggs

Cook the eggs and steak at the same time. Wipe the frying pan clean and place the griddle over a high heat to get hot.

Add the remaining 4 teaspoons of oil to the frying pan, place over a medium heat, crack in the eggs and leave to fry until they turn crispy and brown around the edges.

Steaks

Open the window so any smoke can escape. Rub the steaks with a little oil and season well on both sides. Lay the steaks on the griddle and cook ferociously, without moving them, for 1 minute, then flip over and cook for a further minute on the other side. That's it, they're done.

Spoon a pile of mushrooms onto each plate, top with the steaks, then the eggs.

Or try...

Make steak, mushroom and egg sandwiches – in rolls, baps or even in flour tortillas for a mid-morning snack.

Swap the steaks for burger patties and add slices of cheese for fun.

Great food is often born out of necessity. You'll be amazed by what checking the back of your store cupboard, having a rummage in your fridge or using up the rest of last night's roast can bring. These recipes aren't complicated; they're just delicious.

stores and leftovers

Tomato and Pesto Tarts

I have always been a sucker for anything cooked in, or with, puff pastry. These deep tarts are topped with the concentrated flavour of sweet tomatoes and the kick of a punchy pesto. Serve with peppery watercress. If you like, just make smaller individual ones as snacks for your hungry hordes.

Makes 4 tarts*

500g block puff pastry (all-butter, if possible)

plain flour, for dusting

1 egg, beaten

2 tablespoons pesto (see page 160 for home-made, or just use a jar)

8 plum tomatoes, sliced

salt and freshly ground black pepper

To serve

100g watercress

10ml peppery olive oil

* 1 each as a starter

Prep the pastry

Heat the oven to 220°C/gas 7. Line a baking sheet with baking paper.

On a lightly floured worktop, roll the puff pastry out until it is about 2cm thick. You will need to cut four circular discs from the pastry so you need to find a small plate or saucer that's about 16cm in diameter to use as a template. Place the plate over the pastry and run a sharp knife around the edge to cut out the first disc. Repeat until you have four.

Now you need to lightly score a margin about 1.5–2cm in from the edge of the pastry discs, so find a smaller plate or bowl that you can use as a template. Place the smaller plate in the centre of each pastry disc and lightly run a sharp knife around the edge, being careful not to cut all the way through.

Lift the disks onto the baking sheet and brush with the beaten egg. With a fork, prick the inner circle but not the outer edge – this will stop the pastry from rising in the middle but will allow the outer edge of the tart to rise up.

Build the tarts

Take a good amount of the pesto and spread it over the inner circle of each tart. Place the tops and bottoms of the tomatoes in the centre of the tarts, then start to lay the slices on top of the pesto so they overlap and create a swirl effect – it should look a bit like a Catherine wheel. Season with salt and pepper.

Place the tarts in the oven and bake for 20–25 minutes, until well risen and coloured. Mix the watercress with the olive oil and serve with the tarts.

Tip

Cut out pastry discs, stack them between layers of cling film and keep them in the freezer – ready in case of an emergency! Just take them out of the freezer 10 minutes before you want to cook them, then make the tarts and bake as above.

Panzanella

I have great admiration for the Italians, their love of vegetables and their desire to use every last thing. This is a delicious salad and it uses up all your old bread. Stale bread does work best but if you're using fresh, use crusty and dense. I 'half peel' my cucumber – meaning I peel away strips of the skin. I find all the skin is a little bitter and no skin means it has little structure.

Makes a big bowl of salad as a side

2 tablespoons white vinegar

100ml warm water

300g hunk of stale or crusty bread, torn into chunks about the size of a thumb

5 vine tomatoes, roughly diced

1 cucumber, half peeled and roughly diced

2 celery sticks, roughly diced

1 red onion, finely sliced

3 tablespoons olive oil

3 tablespoons red wine vinegar

a handful of flat-leaf parsley

salt and freshly ground black pepper

Mix the white vinegar with the warm water, then pour it over the bread and leave it to soak until soft – about 10 minutes.

Put your hand on top of the bread, tip the bowl and drain off any excess water.

In a separate large bowl, add the tomatoes, cucumber, celery and red onion. Season it really well, toss, then add the bread. Mix the olive oil and red wine vinegar together and pour over the bread and tomato mixture and toss it again. You must get your hands in there for this bit.

Tear up the parsley and mix it into the salad then transfer the salad to a beautiful serving plate.

Vegetable and Pearl Barley Soup

Pearl barley is a wonderful staple for the store cupboard. It's versatile and takes very little time to cook, yet in my opinion it's underrated and underused. The pearls love to soak up flavour so give them plenty of seasoning and a decent strong stock base. This is a hearty and really healthy soup for any time of the year.

Feeds 4

1 litre vegetable stock or 2 stock cubes dissolved in water

75g pearl barley

50g butter

1 large onion, cut into 5mm dice

2 potatoes, peeled and cut into chunky dice (about 1.5cm)

1 large leek, trimmed and cut into chunky dice (about 1.5cm)

2 large carrots, peeled and cut into chunky dice (about 1.5cm)

4 celery sticks, cut into chunky dice (about 1.5cm)

3 cabbage leaves, shredded (optional)

50ml olive oil

sea salt and white pepper

crusty bread and lashings of butter, to serve

Put half the stock into a small saucepan over a medium heat with the pearl barley and bring it to the boil. Reduce to a simmer and cook for 15 minutes. Then take the pan off the heat and leave the barley sitting in the stock.

Place the butter in a casserole over a medium heat and drop in the onion and potatoes and 3 tablespoons of water, this will help to soften the vegetables and stop them from colouring. Cook them for a good 5 minutes stirring a few times, then add the leek, carrots and celery and cook in the same way for 5 minutes more. Season with white pepper but just a pinch of salt.

Now add the other half of the stock and bring it to a rapid boil. Reduce the heat to a simmer and cook for 20 minutes until the potatoes and carrots are tender. Test with the point of a sharp knife.

When the vegetables are soft add the cooked pearl barley and its cooking stock and bring to the boil. Taste and season if you need to. Drop in the shredded cabbage, if you are using it, and return to the boil, but cook for 2 minutes only. Stir in the olive oil then take the pan off the heat. Serve in generous bowls or mugs with crusty bread and butter on the side.

Herb and Cheese Soufflé Omelette

An omelette is delicious at any time of the day and this magic little number is not only oozing with cheese and speckled with a scattering of herbs, it's puffed up and pillowy. The whipped egg white makes the whole thing rise, like a soufflé. Light and fluffy and cheesy – yum.

Makes 1 omelette but feeds 2

60g butter

6 button mushrooms, sliced

3 eggs

a selection of herbs, such as a few sprigs each of chervil, chives, flat-leaf parsley, tarragon and oregano, each chopped separately (don't chop the herbs too finely)

50g Gruyère, grated

salt and freshly ground black pepper

In an omelette pan, heat half the butter and gently fry the mushrooms with a little salt and pepper over a medium heat for a minute or two, just until they go a little nutty. Spoon the mushrooms onto a plate, leaving as much butter in the pan as possible.

Separate the eggs. Break the yolks with a fork. Whisk the whites until stiff, then gently fold the yolks into the whites until mixed and season well.

Put the omelette pan back over a medium heat, add the rest of the butter and when it starts to bubble, pour the egg mix into the pan and throw in most of the herbs. Stir until the omelette starts to set but is still slightly wobbly in the middle.

Sprinkle with the Gruyère and the mushrooms and cook for another minute to let the omelette rise a little. Fold the omelette by tilting the pan and shuffling the omelette forward – it should roll up like a cigar. Slide onto a warm plate, cut in half and finish with the remaining herbs.

Ramp it up...

You could also fill your omelette with chopped or shredded ham, smoked salmon and cream cheese, a spoonful of horseradish, a sprinkle of paprika, crispy bits of chorizo or mozzarella and basil.

Soda Bread

This bread is very quick and easy to make because it doesn't use yeast and the dough is simply mixed and then baked. Don't handle the dough too much or the bread will become tough – I just shape each loaf gently with my hands. Once the bread is baked it pulls apart or crumbles a little when sliced, which is what I like. Soda bread is ace served with cheese, ham, smoked salmon or soup and it also keeps very well.

Makes 1 good-sized loaf

oil, for greasing

275g strong white flour, plus extra for dusting

200g wholemeal flour

1 generous teaspoon bicarbonate of soda

pinch of salt

420ml buttermilk

1 teaspoon clear honey

Heat the oven to 190°C/gas 5. Grease a baking sheet and dust it with flour.

In a large bowl, stir together the flours, bicarbonate of soda and salt.

Measure the buttermilk in a measuring jug and whisk in the honey. Pour the buttermilk mixture into the flour mixture and stir with a wooden spoon to bring the mix together to form a dough.

Slap the dough down on the greased baking sheet and shape it into a round loaf. Sprinkle with a little flour and use a knife to score a cross in the top of the loaf.

Bake for 35–40 minutes. The bread is ready when it sounds hollow when tapped on the bottom. Leave the bread to cool on a wire rack before slicing, if you can, otherwise just pull a little off and spread it with butter.

Pesto and Pods

My respect for frozen peas and pods is well documented – little beats the ease of opening a bag of frozen peas, broad beans and soya beans. It's not cheating, it's just sensible store cupboard shopping. Yes you can buy pesto – you can use up your store cupboard jar in this recipe – but I love to make my own as the fresh sauce is lush. It's also just really easy – I make mine in a mortar and pestle so you don't need any fancy equipment, and if you need another reason – it freezes really well, so you'll have it in store to accompany those bags of frozen pods.

Feeds 6–8

For the pesto

200g basil, leaves picked

50g pine nuts, toasted

2 garlic cloves, peeled

200g flat-leaf parsley, leaves picked

150ml olive oil

juice of ½ lemon

100g Parmesan, grated

salt and freshly ground black pepper

For the pods

200g frozen peas

100g frozen broad beans

100g sugar snap peas

100g mangetout

100g runner beans, trimmed and cut in half lengthways

100g frozen soya beans

2 spring onions, sliced

Make the pesto*

In a mortar, put a few basil leaves and sprinkle over some of the pine nuts. Pound. When this has reduced in size, add as much of the basil leaves as will fit, some more pine nuts and the garlic and pound again. When all the basil has been pounded, add the parsley and do the same, until it has reduced right down.

Now add the oil, then the lemon juice, then the cheese, pounding after each addition. Bit by bit the pesto will come together. Season well.

Cook the pods

Bring a large pot of water to the boil, drop in all the vegetables and simmer for 4 minutes, or until tender but still crunchy. Drain and leave for 2 minutes and then mix with 2 tablespoons of the pesto. Any pesto you don't use can either be frozen or kept in the fridge for a few days' time.

* You can use a food processor to make the pesto. Put everything except the olive oil and lemon juice in the bowl and pulse it until it's rough, then add the lemon and oil, and pulse again to make a paste.

The Bestest Tomato Sauce for Pasta

This is the quickest sauce I know how to make. It can be used with any pasta you wish, but the bigger the better, and please, please serve it with loads of cheese. There's a lot of olive oil in the sauce for a reason – it should be opulent and rich to celebrate the amazing flavour of fruity ripe tomatoes.

Feeds 4–6

100ml olive oil

1 onion, diced

1 garlic clove, crushed

1 teaspoon sea salt

1 teaspoon ground black pepper

700g very ripe tomatoes, chopped

400g dried pasta (I like rigatoni)

loads of Parmesan, to serve

Heat the oil in a large heavy-based pan over a medium heat. Add the onion and cook for a few minutes, stirring all the time, then add the garlic, salt and pepper and cook for a couple of minutes more. Add the chopped tomatoes and squash them down with the back of a spoon into the onion mixture and bring to the boil, then turn the heat down to a very gentle simmer and cook for a good 10 minutes, stirring every so often until you've got tomato sauce.

Cook the pasta in boiling salted water according to the packet instructions. Drain it quickly but keep it wet. Drop the pasta into the boiling sauce, and bring to the boil so that sauce and pasta become one. Stir well. Serve with lashings of Parmesan.

Use it later...

Any sauce that you don't use can be kept in the fridge for a few days. Or freeze it.

Pasta e Fagioli

The great soups of Italy are highly seasoned and full of big, beautiful chunks of vegetables and meat. Some are served with bread; others have bread floating on top; many contain dried beans and pasta. This rich soup, translated as 'pasta and beans', is one such classic. I was taught to make it by an Italian lady who used to work with me in Australia. She also taught me an Italian saying: 'Don't boil the love out of it.' What she meant was simmer things rather than boil them. I can hear her saying it as I write.

Serves 6

2 carrots, peeled

2 onions

2 long celery sticks

3 tomatoes

100ml olive oil, plus extra to serve (optional)

100g rindless smoked or unsmoked bacon (it's up to you), roughly chopped

1 x 400g tin borlotti beans (don't drain them)

1 x 400g tin haricot beans (don't drain them)

1 litre vegetable stock (use stock cubes)

150g macaroni

salt and freshly ground black pepper

To serve

100g pesto (see page 160 if you want to make your own)

shaved Parmesan

Cut the vegetables into soup-sized pieces – you know, hunky chunks that fit on a spoon.

Heat the oil in a large pan over a medium heat. Throw in the bacon and the onion, cook for 5 minutes or until coloured, then add the veg and cook for 5 minutes more, stirring occasionally. Season with salt and pepper.

Add the beans, water and all, pour in the vegetable stock and bring to the boil. Simmer for a good 5 minutes. Taste and adjust the seasoning if necessary. Add the macaroni and cook for at least another 15 minutes, or until it's soft. The pasta thickens the soup, as do the beans.

Ladle the soup into large bowls, drop a spoonful of pesto on top of each and top with Parmesan shavings. Pour over some olive oil if you wish.

Rösti

By definition a rösti is made and cooked with raw potato, but this recipe is one that I have honed over the years. By pouring boiling water over the grated raw potato it scalds it and washes away some of the starch, so the cooking is just a little less temperamental and quicker. Some might say it's not a true rösti but in my books, if it works, go for it.

Makes a big thick one*

For the Greek salad

75ml extra virgin olive oil

25ml red wine vinegar

200g feta cheese, diced

1 small cucumber, de-seeded and diced

a handful of flat-leaf parsley leaves

100g large pitted green olives, squashed with the flat of your hand

3 large plum tomatoes, roughly chopped

For the rösti

2 large roasting potatoes, peeled and coarsely grated

1 small onion, sliced

500ml boiling water from the kettle

2 thyme sprigs, leaves picked

50g butter, melted

2 tablespoons vegetable oil

salt and freshly ground black pepper

Make the Greek salad

Whisk the oil and vinegar until you have a smooth dressing.

Mix all the remaining bits for the Greek Salad in a bowl, toss with the dressing and set aside to mature while you make the rosti.

Make the rosti

Mix the grated potatoes and onions in a mixing bowl. Pour over the 500ml of boiling water from the kettle and leave the mixture to sit for 2 minutes, then drain. This softens the potatoes and washes out any excess starch. Press it down to get rid of any extra water, then season really well and stir in the thyme and melted butter.

Cook them

Take a large deep frying pan (or two smaller ones) and heat the oil. Drop the potato mix into the pan and use a spatula to flatten it out like a pancake. Keep the heat low and cook for 5 minutes, at least. The edges should start to brown and if you shake the pan the potato should move around.

When it's brown, turn the rösti over to cook the other side for about another 5 minutes or so – it should be golden brown and crisp on the outside but fluffy inside. Serve topped with some of the Greek salad and plenty more on the side.

Serve...

* or 2 thinner ones, to feed a family of 4

With whatever you wish, from fried eggs to ham and cheese. And if you make thin ones, roll them up with a frankfurter inside. Bad I know, but I never said anything about healthy food!

Potato and Goat's Cheese Croquettes with Almond Crumbs

Posh and a little bit clever but also really tasty. The inspiration for this is crumbed and fried Camembert, all hot and gooey and coated in crumbs. With crispy almond crumbs, these croquettes are even better.

Makes 12–16

For the croquettes

1kg potatoes, peeled and cut into even-sized pieces

50g butter

4 teaspoons milk

1 egg yolk

150g soft goat's cheese

plain flour, for dusting

1.5 litres vegetable oil, for frying

salt and freshly ground white pepper

For the almond crumbs

100g plain flour

2 eggs, beaten

a splash of milk

50g flaked almonds, crushed

Prep and shape the croquettes

Put the potatoes into a large saucepan, cover with cold water and add a teaspoon of salt. Bring to the boil and simmer for 20 minutes, until soft. Drain, then put them back in the pot covered with a tea towel for about 5 minutes, so they dry out. While they are still hot, mash them with a fork until they are fluffy with no lumps.

Now put the mash back over a low heat. Push the mash to one side of the pot, pour the butter and milk into the other side and season with some salt and pepper. When the butter starts to melt, beat everything together. When it's smooth and steaming, take it off the heat. Mix in the egg yolk, then crumble over the goat's cheese.

The potato needs to be warm while you do the next bit. Scatter your worktop with a little flour and divide the mix into four balls. Take a potato ball and roll it into a snake (like you did with playdough when you were a child); it should be the diameter of a 50 pence piece. Repeat with the other three balls, then cut each one into 6cm lengths. Dust lightly with flour and leave to cool.

Make the almond crumbs

Lay out three dishes, put the flour into the first, mix the beaten eggs with the milk in the second and put the crushed almonds into the third.

Roll each croquette first in the flour, then in the egg, and finally in the crushed almonds, making sure each croquette is well coated at each stage or they will explode in the oil. Chill for 30 minutes.

Fry the croquettes

Pour the oil into a wok or deep pan (or use a deep fat fryer) and heat to 170°C – it will start to shimmer. Deep-fry the croquettes, about four at a time, rolling them every minute or so, until they are golden – this should take about 4–5 minutes. Drain on kitchen paper and keep to one side while you fry the rest.

Sausage and Bean Casserole

It is true that I am a proud dad and I love to watch my kids clean their plates, so over the years I have had many a consultation with them on the sort of dishes they would like to eat. This is a very special one and it's actually the first time I have thought about it being a recipe.

Will feed 6 youngsters*

2 tablespoons vegetable oil

12 really big, thick pork sausages

1 onion, diced

2 large potatoes, peeled and diced

2 carrots, peeled and diced

1 x 400g tin white beans, such as cannellini or haricot (don't drain them)

1 x 400g tin chopped tomatoes

200ml water

salt and freshly ground black pepper

* or 4 growing teens (maybe)

Turn the oven to 180°C/gas 4.

Heat a large casserole over a high heat. Add the oil, then the sausages, and leave them to colour a little on each side – this should take 4–5 minutes.

Add the onion and potato and give the pan a really good stir. Leave to cook for a couple of minutes and then stir again so nothing sticks. Once the onion and potato have coloured a little, add the carrots and season. Stir again and let the carrots cook for a few more minutes.

Now pour in the beans, including their liquid, the tomatoes and the extra water. Bring to the boil and when bubbling scrape the bottom of the casserole so it doesn't stick. Pop the lid on and put the casserole in the oven. Cook for 30 minutes.

Take the lid off, turn the heat up to 220°C/gas 7 and cook for a further 15 minutes – the top should colour and go a bit crispy. Dig in.

Try...

My kids like this served in different ways: on hot buttered toast; with a few eggs cracked into it at the end then baked for a bit longer, until the eggs are cooked through; even with macaroni cheese.

Dried Mushroom and Parmesan Risotto

The best Arborio rice is highly polished and has a chalky stripe down each grain, which indicates it contains a lot of starch – just what you need for a good risotto. Putting some dried ceps into a bag of rice for a while before using it gives the rice a lovely smoky, mushroom flavour.

Makes a pot, enough for 4

40g dried ceps or mixed dried mushrooms

1 litre hot stock (use stock cubes – veg, chicken or porcini)

45g butter

1 tablespoon olive oil

2 banana shallots (or a small onion), diced

350g Arborio rice

75g Parmesan, grated

a handful of freshly chopped flat-leaf parsley

Soak the mushrooms in boiling water for 10 minutes, then drain.

Get the stock simmering; the rice and the stock should be at about the same temperature. If they're not the rice might become a bit cloggy on the outside but not be cooked inside.

In a large pan, heat 15g of the butter and the oil. Add the shallots and cook over a medium heat for a few minutes, until softened. Drain the mushrooms, add the mushrooms to the pan and give them a good stir. When it all starts to sizzle add the rice. Give it a good stir. Now start to add the hot stock, a ladleful at a time. After each addition, stir the pan and let the stock come to the boil. After 15–20 minutes the rice will be fluffy and the whole thing should be brown and sticky. Take the pan off the heat, add the Parmesan and the remaining butter and whisk the rice like mad so that it becomes creamy. Throw in the parsley, stir well and serve.

Or...

Adapt this recipe in lots of different ways: add chopped butternut squash at the start of the cooking or cooked prawns at the end; use fresh mushrooms instead of dried ones if you have them; replace the Parmesan with a little goat's cheese, or sprinkle toasted pine nuts or pumpkin seeds over the top of the finished dish.

Vegetable Tagine

When I first started to make tagines all those years ago buying harissa was almost impossible. Today it's widely available in supermarkets and delis, so why not buy it? Although this recipe has a long-ish list of ingredients, most are store-cupboard staples and you can use whatever veg you want, adjusting the cooking time a little as necessary. Serve it with whatever you like; I like preserved lemon strips and loads of chopped mint, harissa and, if I'm in the mood, some flatbreads.

Feeds 6

2 carrots, peeled, cut in half lengthways and then cut in half the other way

2 large parsnips, peeled, cut in half lengthways and then cut in half the other way

2 red onions, halved

2 large potatoes, peeled and quartered

3 leeks (white parts only), split, washed and cut into 6cm lengths

30ml olive oil

400ml water

12 dried prunes, dates or figs

2 preserved lemons (optional)

small jar of harissa (or make your own, see page 198), to serve

2 sprigs of mint, leaves picked and chopped, to serve

For the chermoula (marinade)

1 tablespoon ground cumin

1 tablespoon ground paprika

1 tablespoon ground turmeric

1 teaspoon hot chilli powder

2 large red onions, roughly chopped

3 garlic cloves

3.5cm piece of fresh root ginger, peeled and roughly chopped

200ml olive oil

200ml lemon juice (the juice of about 3 lemons)

1 generous tablespoon honey

a large handful of flat-leaf parsley

a large handful of coriander

For the couscous

300g couscous

100g butter, cut into cubes

a small handful of sultanas

salt and freshly ground black pepper

Vegetable Tagine

Make the chermoula

Heat a frying pan over a high heat, add the spices, turn off the heat and let them toast, stirring them a bit until they brown. Put the toasted spices and all the remaining ingredients in a food-processor and blitz to a paste.

Marinate the veg

Put the carrots, parsnips, red onions, potatoes and leeks in a large bowl, pour over the chermoula, mix with your fingers and marinate for an hour or so.

Cook the tagine

Heat the oven to 220°C/gas 7. Heat the olive oil in a large frying pan over a medium–high heat and brown the marinated leeks and potatoes quickly on all sides.

Transfer to a tagine or large casserole along with the rest of the marinated veg and add the dried fruit. Pour over the water – it should cover the veg by about 1cm; add more if necessary. Cover the tagine or casserole with a lid, place in the oven and cook for about 45 minutes, then turn the oven down to 180°C/gas 4 and cook for another 45 minutes.

Make the couscous

A good 15 minutes before the tagine is ready, make the couscous. Rinse the couscous in cold water and then pour it into a shallow bowl. Season with a good amount of salt and pepper, scatter the butter over the top and sprinkle the sultanas around the edge of the bowl. Pour boiling water over the top until the couscous is covered by about 1cm. Cover with a plate and leave for 10–15 minutes; the grains will plump up and become tender. Uncover and run a fork through it. Keep warm.

Almost there...

Meanwhile, if using the preserved lemons, cut the rind off and slice into thin strips (discard the mush).

Take the tagine out of the oven straight to the table. Serve the couscous, harissa, mint and lemon strips separately alongside. Open the tagine and let everyone dive in and help themselves to the bits.

You can see it in all its glory on the next page...

Glamorgan Sausages

My search for a great vegetarian sausage recipe took me far and wide, from Australia to Asia to Ireland, with Europe in between. I finally stumbled across these little beauties closer to home – in Wales. They're simply made with some cheese, breadcrumbs and a couple of eggs and they are grand. To my mind, they taste a bit like the stuffing you get from a good chicken. They are moreish, so beware.

Feeds 4

175g Caerphilly cheese or Cheshire cheese, grated

225g fresh breadcrumbs

1 banana shallot, grated

1 tablespoon chopped flat-leaf parsley

1 tablespoon chopped chives

1 egg, beaten

20ml milk

1 teaspoon hot English mustard

plain flour, for dusting

300ml vegetable oil, for frying

salt and freshly ground black pepper

jar of apple sauce or apple chutney, to serve

For the coating

1 egg, beaten

50ml milk

50g plain flour

1 teaspoon paprika

Prep the sausage mixture

In a large bowl, mix the cheese, breadcrumbs, shallot and herbs and season with salt and pepper.

In a jug, beat together the egg, milk and mustard. Pour the egg mixture over the cheesy breadcrumbs and mash together until you get a dough.

On a lightly floured worktop, roll out the mix into long sausages roughly 2cm thick and then cut the sausages into 8cm lengths – you should get about eight.

Coat them

Beat the egg and milk together in a shallow dish. Spread out the flour in another dish and season with the paprika. Roll the sausages in the egg mixture and then in the seasoned flour. Leave on a tray in the fridge for 10 minutes to set.

Cook the sausages

Heat the oil in a heavy-based frying pan and gently fry the sausages over a medium heat for about 4–5 minutes, turning, until brown all over. Drain well on kitchen paper. Serve with apple sauce or apple chutney.

For a non-vego version

Add bits of crisp bacon, flaked smoked haddock or shredded ham and chopped-up peas to the sausage mixture and then coat and cook as above.

Fried Rice

Many of us think of fried rice as something that is eaten with other Chinese takeaway dishes. Yes it is, but making it yourself is also a great way of using up leftover cooked rice (I always make too much). My cupboard is never without a jar of chilli black bean sauce and a bottle of sweet chilli sauce so I liberally spoon one of them over this at the end.

For 2 as a main or 4 as a side

2 tablespoons vegetable oil

1 thumb-sized piece of fresh root ginger, peeled and grated

2 garlic cloves, grated

1 long red chilli, de-seeded (if you don't want it hot) and diced

20ml sesame oil

500g cooked rice

30g frozen peas

2 spring onions, sliced

30ml soya sauce

2 eggs

Heat the vegetable oil in a wok or large frying pan. When hot, add the ginger and garlic and slowly fry over a low heat until fragrant – don't colour them.

Now add the chilli and sesame oil and turn up the heat. Add the rice, break it up and stir it around really well for a good 4–5 minutes, scraping the base of the pan or wok so that the rice doesn't burn (the rice will heat all the way through and it sort of pops). Add the peas and give everything a really good stir so the peas cook. Stir in the spring onions and cook for 2 minutes. Add the soy sauce.

Break the eggs into the rice and give them a good stir. Turn the heat up as high as you can, then really scrape the bottom of the wok. Stir for a minute, then take the wok off the heat, leave to stand for a minute and then give it another stir. And that's it: fried rice.

Or try...

Add raw prawns, chicken or slivers of pork to the oil with the garlic and chilli or finish the dish with stir-fried prawns, chicken or slivers of pork on top.

Chicken and Stuffing Rolls

This is more of a concept than a recipe but it's just such a great way of using up leftovers that it had to go in the book. A soft warm roll filled with chicken and stuffing, lashings of butter and warmed through is simply the best type of food.

Makes 2

2 long soft rolls

lots of butter

leftover stuffing, cold or hot

leftover roast chicken, stripped from the bone, cold or hot

mayonnaise

Heat the oven to 180°C/gas 4.

Split the rolls down the middle and butter them liberally. Fill each roll with a line of stuffing, then a line of chicken and spread a little mayonnaise over the chicken.

Lay two pieces of kitchen foil on a worktop and sprinkle with a little water (the water keeps the rolls soft when they're heated). Wrap the stuffed rolls in the foil and put in the oven for 10 minutes.

Or try...

Once the rolls are hot, you can add all sorts of bits and pieces to them: watercress, rocket, coleslaw, iceberg lettuce, Little Gem lettuce, pea shoots or maybe even some corn relish. Try the same with slices of roast beef and gravy.

Ham Croquettes

Be careful, these croquettes are addictive. Once you've started, someone may come home and find you sat in the corner surrounded by crumbs from these wonderful little morsels. But if you can keep your hands off them for long enough, they stay hot for a good 10 minutes once they're out of the oil so are brilliant as little party snacks. I have also recently discovered that you can buy pre-shredded ham hock in supermarkets. Result.

Makes 26

1 small banana shallot or ½ small onion, chopped

50g butter

50g plain flour, plus an extra large handful for coating

300ml milk

300g cooked ham, smoked ham or ham hock (or a mixture), shredded

150g firm mozzarella, grated

1 tablespoon Dijon mustard

1 tablespoon chopped flat-leaf parsley

2 eggs, beaten

50g dried breadcrumbs

1.5 litres vegetable oil, for frying

salt and freshly ground black pepper

Make the croquettes

Put the shallot and butter in a small pan and cook over a low heat until the shallot is soft but not coloured. Add the flour, stir with a whisk and cook until it becomes a paste (this is called a roux). Pour in the milk, whisking like mad, and bring to the boil, then turn the heat down to a simmer and cook for about 10 minutes. Take the pan off the heat.

Add the ham, mozzarella, mustard and parsley and season well with salt and pepper. Pour the mixture into a tray or bowl and leave in the fridge for about 30 minutes to cool and form a thick paste.

When it's cool, shape the croquettes by rolling enough mixture between your palms to form golf-ball-sized balls.

Crumb the croquettes

Lay out three plates: one with the handful of flour, one with the beaten eggs and one with the breadcrumbs, in that order. Roll the croquettes in the flour, then in the eggs and finally in the breadcrumbs, making sure each croquette is well coated at each stage. Line up the croquettes on a tray and put them in the fridge for a good hour to set.

Cook the croquettes

Heat the oil in a wok or deep saucepan (or use a deep fat fryer) to 170°C – or throw in a breadcrumb; it should sizzle. Deep-fry the croquettes in two to three batches, until they float to the top of the oil and are golden – this should take about 4–5 minutes. Let these delicious little croquettes cool a little before eating because they get really, really hot.

Dad's Roast Lamb Fritters

Dad always cooked these fritters the day after we had feasted on roast lamb. They are really easy to make, quick and cheap. I don't know where the recipe originated but my dad used to cook them for me and my brothers and they bring back many happy memories of growing up. I love them. And him.

Makes about 8–10 fritters

500g roast lamb, fat trimmed off and diced into pieces the size of your thumb

1 small onion, finely diced

300g self-raising flour

1 teaspoon salt

350ml cold water

vegetable oil, for frying

freshly ground black pepper

Heat the oven to 160°C/gas 3.

Mix together the lamb and onion. In a separate large bowl, mix together the flour, salt, some pepper and water. Drop the lamb and onion into the flour and mix well.

You will need to cook the fritters in at least two batches. Pour a good layer of oil into a large frying pan – it should be about 0.5cm deep. Drop large tablespoonfuls of the fritter mixture into the oil. These little morsels are cooked in the same way as a pancake – slowly, over a medium heat for 3–4 minutes, until brown around the edges. Turn the heat down if the fritters cook too frantically. Turn the fritters over and leave to cook for another few minutes until they're brown and crispy.

Move the cooked fritters into a roasting tin and pop them in the oven to keep warm while you cook the remaining batch(es).

Serve...

As a whole meal with creamed spinach, peas, beans and buttered carrots or as a snack with piccalilli, mustard, tomato or brown sauce.

Spaghetti Carbonara

This has to be my all-time favourite pasta dish and I have eaten variations all over the world. It is my go-to recipe when I get home and find I have little in the fridge but want to eat something delicious. I make it a lot. Most of us have bacon, eggs and a little cheese in the fridge and a packet of spaghetti in the cupboard, so it's easily earned its place in this chapter.

Feeds 4–6*

1 tablespoon sea salt

1 tablespoon olive oil

500g spaghetti

2 tablespoons vegetable oil

250g smoked streaky bacon or pancetta, cut into batons

1 teaspoon freshly ground black pepper, or more if you're me

3 large eggs

100g Parmesan, grated, plus an extra hunk to serve

a handful of flat-leaf parsley, chopped

* I always make too much

Boil a large pan of water, adding the salt and olive oil and cook the spaghetti according to the packet instructions.

Heat a large frying pan over a high heat and add the vegetable oil. Throw in the bacon or pancetta and leave to sizzle for 3 minutes, stirring every so often. Continue to cook for a couple more minutes, making sure the bacon is frying and making a sizzling noise. Add the pepper – lots of it.

Break the eggs into a bowl and bust the yolks with a fork but don't beat them.

When the spaghetti is cooked and the bacon is crispy use a pair of tongs to lift the spaghetti out of the water straight into the pan of sizzling bacon. Toss it well and cook for 1 minute, keeping the heat really high. Add the eggs and the grated Parmesan and toss again. Take the pan off the heat and leave to stand for a minute or so – the residual heat will cook the eggs.

Sprinkle with the parsley and serve in a big bowl in the middle of the table. Let people serve themselves, and give them a hunk of Parmesan and a grater to be as greedy as they like.

Corn Dogs and Coleslaw

Corn dogs are a favourite in Australia, where they are called Pluto Pups, and they are always dipped in lots and lots of tomato sauce. These are both good and bad – yin and yang, shall we say. They probably aren't the healthiest dogs but I have to say they taste really, really good.

Serves 4–8

For the coleslaw

1 small green cabbage, shredded

2 largish carrots, peeled and grated

1 long red chilli, de-seeded and diced

juice of 1 lemon

1 tablespoon crème fraîche

2 teaspoons roasted sesame seeds

12 cherry tomatoes, halved

a handful each of mint and coriander, chopped

salt and freshly ground black pepper

For the dogs

150ml milk

2 eggs, beaten

30ml vegetable oil

2 tablespoons sugar

1 teaspoon salt

100g self-raising flour, plus extra for coating

2 teaspoons baking powder

150g polenta or cornmeal

8 jumbo frankfurters

2 litres vegetable oil, for frying

Make the coleslaw

Put the cabbage, carrots and chilli in a large bowl, season with salt and pepper, squeeze over the lemon juice and leave to stand for 10 minutes. Stir in the crème fraîche and all the rest of the ingredients and mix well. It can now be stored in the fridge for hours.

Coat the dogs

In a large bowl, mix together the milk, eggs, oil, sugar and salt and leave to stand for a couple of minutes – the salt breaks down the egg and makes it all more liquid. Drop in the flour, baking powder and polenta and whisk to a batter.

Put a good amount of flour on a plate. Take your frankfurters and coat them completely in the flour – the batter won't stick to the hot dogs unless they are coated. Shove skewers lengthways into the floured franks.

Fry the dogs

Pour the oil into a wok or deep pan (or use a deep fat fryer) and heat the oil to 180°C.

Pour a good amount of the batter onto a plate and roll the floured franks in it so they are well coated in the batter.

Holding the skewer, lower two of the battered franks into the hot oil, turn and cook gently for a good 5 minutes, until coloured all over. Drain well on kitchen paper. Fry two at a time, bringing the oil back to temperature between each batch. Serve with the coleslaw and tomato sauce.

Prawn and Pineapple Curry

This might sound like a bit of an odd one but it is one of my favourite summer curries. You can buy dried or even frozen Kaffir lime leaves but if they're not in your store cupboard just use half a lime. The palm sugar can be substituted with soft brown sugar and you can leave the fish sauce out and just make sure you season well with salt.

Feeds 6

50ml vegetable oil

50g Thai red curry paste (make sure you buy the one in the plastic tub, or make your own, see page 102)

1 tablespoon palm sugar (or soft brown sugar if you don't have palm sugar)

2 teaspoons fish sauce

2 x 400g tins coconut milk

1 pineapple, peeled, cored and chopped into large chunks

200ml water

10 Kaffir lime leaves, torn

3 large red chillies, halved lengthways and de-seeded

3 lemongrass stalks

500g raw prawns, peeled but leave the tails on

a handful of coriander, roughly chopped

rice or noodles, to serve

In a heavy-based pan, heat the oil over a medium heat and add the curry paste. Fry the paste until fragrant, then add the sugar and stir well. The paste will start to caramelise and smell very strong – this is just what you want.

Add the fish sauce and cook until the mixture turns a dark colour. Add the coconut milk and pineapple and bring to the boil. Add the water and bring back to the boil. Add the torn lime leaves, chilli and lemongrass.

Simmer for 10 minutes, until fragrant and the pineapple is translucent, then add the prawns and bring back to the boil. Cook for about 2 minutes, or until the prawns turn pink. Take off the heat, scatter over the coriander and eat! It should be soupy and sweet and hot all at the same time. Serve with lots of rice or noodles.

When the sun shines I move the feast outside.
British weather doesn't always allow you to
stay there for as long as you might want but
that doesn't matter; move indoors if you
have to. The feast just needs to be plentiful
and long-lasting.

all
outside

Spring Salad

Spring is a great time for vegetables so let's celebrate them and eat them in quantity. A salad like this needs a good dressing and this one is a beaut – I always make more than I need, as does this recipe, so do as I do and store the extra in a jar in the fridge ready for whatever and whenever you need it.

Feeds 10 as a side

10 asparagus spears, sliced into 7cm lengths at an angle

150g broad beans

150g soya beans

150g fresh or frozen peas

3 spring onions, sliced into 7.5cm lengths at an angle

olive oil, for drizzling

15 mint leaves, 10 leaves torn and 5 leaves shredded

salt and freshly ground black pepper

For the dressing

1 tablespoon Dijon mustard

75ml red wine vinegar

300ml extra virgin olive oil

1 teaspoon walnut oil

sea salt

Get the veg sorted

Bring a large pan of salted water to the boil. Drop in the asparagus, bring the water back to the boil, then add the broad beans, soya beans, peas and spring onions. Bring back to the boil until they are cooked. Drain and cool quickly under cold running water.

Spread the cooked vegetables on a tray and place in the fridge for 10 minutes to cool. Sprinkle the veg with a little olive oil and season with salt and pepper.

Make the dressing

Spoon the mustard and vinegar into a small bowl and whisk until blended. Slowly pour in the oils, whisking all the time, until the dressing is thickish (like a sauce). Season with a good whack of sea salt and black pepper.

Put the chilled veg in a pretty serving dish, add the mint (torn and shredded) and mix together, then splatter with some dressing.

Or try...

Sprinkle some pecorino shavings over the top.

Chickpea Salad

Chickpeas, chickpeas everywhere – because I really like them and they come in tins and so are always a great store cupboard stalwart. I have included a recipe for how to make harissa but you can, of course, buy it ready-made from a supermarket or deli. But maybe you'll give it a go?

For 6–8 as a side

For the harissa

3 long red chillies, chopped

2 teaspoons smoked paprika

100ml olive oil

6 garlic cloves, chopped

1 teaspoon ground cumin

salt and freshly ground black pepper

For the salad

2 x 400g tins chickpeas, drained

small bunch of mint, leaves picked

small bunch of coriander, leaves picked

small bunch of flat-leaf parsley, leaves picked

2 red onions, sliced

2 large tomatoes, chopped

juice of 1 lime

plain yoghurt, to serve

To make the harissa*

Put everything in a pan, bring it to the boil and simmer gently for 20 minutes, unti the chillies turn dark red and the garlic starts to toast. Pour it hot into a food processor, blend it to a paste, and then put it back in the pan and cook for another 10 minutes, until it turns dark red and has become a thick paste.

To make the salad

Mix together all the ingredients, except the yoghurt, in a large bowl. Add 2 teaspoons of harissa and stir really well, mashing the salad a little so it's a bit rough and rugged (like me!) Serve with a blob of yoghurt.

*Store any leftover harissa in the fridge for a couple of weeks.

Flatbreads and Tzatziki

When you're having a barbecue, it's only right and proper to set the table and pile flatbreads, salads and sauces in the middle: think yoghurt, chilli sauce, mayonnaise, chopped lettuce and tomatoes, some cucumber and mint; they all work well with grilled fish, meat and vegetables.

These flatbreads are really easy. They can be cooked under a grill or in a hot oven or even over glowing coals. Make sure you watch them carefully, though, as they can change colour quickly.

Feeds 10-12

For the flatbreads (makes 10–12 good-sized breads)

325g plain flour

1 teaspoon salt

1 teaspoon sugar

1 x 7g sachet fast-action yeast

100ml milk

150ml plain yoghurt

60g butter or ghee, melted

sesame seeds (optional)

olive oil, for brushing

For the tzatziki

1 garlic clove

150ml natural yoghurt

10 mint leaves, chopped

1 large cucumber, very finely sliced

juice of 1 lemon

sea salt

Make the dough

Put the flour, salt, sugar and yeast in a large bowl and mix well. Heat the milk until lukewarm. Reserving 1 tablespoon of yoghurt, add the rest to the milk, then add the melted butter or ghee and mix well.

Slowly pour the yoghurt mixture over the flour and mix well. Now knead for about 5 minutes on a well-floured worktop, until you have a springy dough. Cover the bowl with cling film and leave the dough to rise in a warm place for about 1 hour or until doubled in size.

Turn the dough out, slap it and it will shrink. Divide the dough into 10 or 12 even-sized pieces and roll each piece into a ball. Cover with cling film or a clean tea towel and leave to rise for another 15 minutes. Gently flatten the balls of dough into rough teardrop shapes and use a rolling pin to roll them out to about 1cm, and spread with the reserved yoghurt.

Heat the grill to high and put a large baking sheet under it to heat for about 10 minutes.

Make the tzatziki

Using a mortar and pestle, pound the garlic with a little salt to form a paste. Put the yoghurt in a bowl, stir in the garlic paste and mint. Finally, mix together the cucumber and lemon juice, then combine the yoghurt with the cucumber and stir well.

Cook the flatbreads

Place a few flatbreads on the hot baking sheet and grill for 2–3 minutes, then turn over, sprinkle with some sesame seeds, if using, and cook for a further 2–3 minutes.

Repeat until all the flatbreads are cooked, brushing each flatbread with a little olive oil as soon as it is cooked and stacking one on top of each other while hot.

Serve the flatbreads with the tzatzkiki.

Iceberg Lettuce and Blue Cheese Salad

I have no idea why but iceberg is my favourite lettuce in the whole wide world. Don't get me wrong, I like some of the fancy and colourful ones but give me an iceberg any day. This is the simplest salad and I love it!

Use good-quality olive oil, it should be strong and peppery and works a treat with the lettuce and blue cheese.

Feeds 4

1 iceberg lettuce

200g creamy dolcelatte

2 teaspoons olive oil

freshly ground black pepper

Wash the lettuce under cold running water and get rid of the outer leaves. Using a sharp knife, cut the lettuce in half then half again. Use both hands to shake any excess water off the lettuce.

Put each lettuce quarter on a serving plate. Use a fork to crumble the cheese, then dot pieces of the cheese around the lettuce, sprinkle with the olive oil and season with black pepper.

Bulk it out...

Sprinkle crispy bacon over the top of the lettuce.

Replace the dolcelatte with some shaved Parmesan.

Serve the salad with shredded, grilled chicken.

Fry a handful of fresh breadcrumbs in a little bacon fat and sprinkle the toasted breadcrumbs over the salad.

Also nice with tinned anchovies.

Imam Bayildi

This is one of my all-time favourite barbecue sides. It is sloppy and spicy and works well with everything, from simple things like sausages and grilled lamb chops to mushroom and halloumi kebabs and spiced lamb. It's also a great starter served with flatbreads.

Serves 4–6 as a side

3 aubergines, cut into 3cm chunks

2 teaspoons cumin seeds

1 teaspoon coriander seeds

1 cardamom pod, cracked

100ml olive oil

1 teaspoon ground turmeric

3 garlic cloves, roughly chopped

3 very ripe plum tomatoes, chopped

75g sultanas

a good handful of freshly chopped flat-leaf parsley

Bring a large pot of water to the boil, drop in the aubergines and push them under the water. Bring them back to the boil and cook for 2 minutes. Drain in a colander and leave to sit.

Using a mortar and pestle, grind the whole spices to a fine powder. (Alternatively, use ground spices.)

Heat half the oil in a large heavy-based frying pan, add all the ground spices, including the turmeric, and cook for a few minutes until you have an aromatic paste. Add the aubergine and garlic, stir everything around and then let the mixture sit and cook for a few minutes until the aubergine colours nicely on the underside. Use a fish slice to flip the mixture over and leave until the other side colours in the same way. It will take about 3–5 minutes. Add the tomatoes, stir briefly and cook for another 2 minutes, then take the pan off the heat. Stir in the sultanas, leave to cool and then mix in the parsley and the remaining olive oil.

A Real Steak

A double-cut T-Bone has something for everyone: there's a hunk of bone to chew on, a tender fillet, some crispy fat and a lovely slab of tasty sirloin all for the taking. It is an expensive cut, but cooked my way it can feed four people easily.

The chard is my nod to Italy, where I first ate these steaks, but chard is also one of my favourite greens. It can be served hot or cold; it's up to you.

Serves 8

2 large T-bone steaks, about 700g each, at room temperature

30ml vegetable oil

1 teaspoon salt

freshly ground black pepper

For the chard

500g Swiss chard

60g butter, diced

juice of 1 lemon

20g capers

60g anchovies in oil, drained and chopped

20ml olive oil

Tips

Oil the meat, not the pan.

Season the steak after it has been oiled so the salt does not suck the moisture out of the meat.

Let the meat rest after it has been cooked so that it can relax before you carve and serve.

Prep the meat

Light the barbecue. Use a sharp knife to score the fat all the way to the flesh – this will allow the fat and sinew to shrink as it cooks but won't make the meat shrink. Rub the steaks all over with oil and then season liberally with salt and pepper.

Prep the chard

Strip the leaves from the chard, wash and set to one side. Trim the stalks of any bruised bits and then cut into batons. Bring a large pan of salted water to the boil, throw in the stalks and return to the boil. Drop the leaves into the boiling water, pushing them under the surface, and cook for a minute, then drain.

Cook the meat

Put the T-bones, fat-side down, on the barbecue or griddle so that the fat starts to melt. Once the fat begins to melt and char, let the steaks fall naturally to one side and leave to cook for 4 minutes (don't be tempted to move the steak while it is cooking). Turn the steaks over and cook for a further 4 minutes. Now turn the steaks again, rotating them by 180 degrees, and grill for 2 minutes then flip the steaks and cook for another 2 minutes. Take the steaks off the heat and leave to rest for 10 minutes before carving.

Cook the chard

Melt the butter in a large frying pan over a medium heat, then drop in the hot and watery chard and cook for a minute or so. Season the chard, add the lemon juice, capers and anchovies, toss well and then add the olive oil and toss again. Transfer to a bowl.

And relax

When you are ready to serve, sit one steak on its bone, and cut the big hunks of meat off each side of the bone, then slice the meat. Serve the steak with the chard and anchovies. Yum.

The Best-ever Beef Burger

Do you want your burgers to be big and juicy, even if you like them well done? Well, a good burger needs fat. I use minced beef that has a fat content of 30 per cent – I know that may sound like a lot, but you need the fat to keep the meat moist while it cooks. My now not-so-secret ingredients are oyster sauce and tomato sauce.

Makes 8 big burgers
(generous ones)

1.5kg fatty and coarse minced beef (preferably bought from a butcher)

1 tablespoon oyster sauce

1 tablespoon tomato sauce (ketchup if you're not Aussie)

1 egg yolk

a good handful of chopped flat-leaf parsley

For the tomato relish*

40ml vegetable oil

4 garlic cloves, crushed

2 large banana shallots or 1 large onion, sliced

10g salt

2 teaspoons ground cumin

1 teaspoon ground coriander

1 teaspoon smoked paprika

2 x 400g tins chopped tomatoes

250ml white wine vinegar, plus extra if necessary

25g sugar, plus extra if necessary

Make the burger patties

Put the minced beef, oyster sauce, tomato sauce and egg yolk in a large bowl. Using a fork, gently mix it together, then add the parsley and mix again. (You need to mix this gently to keep the texture of the mince.)

Divide the mixture into eight then roll each piece into a large ball. Cut 16 squares of greaseproof paper about the size of your burger bun. Flatten the balls between two slices of the greaseproof until they're about 3cm thick. Lay them on a tray. Put them in the fridge and leave to chill for a good hour, if possible.

Make the tomato relish

Heat the oil in a large pan, then add the garlic, shallots, salt and spices and slowly cook over a low heat for 5 minutes, stirring all the time, until the garlic and shallots are soft. Add the tomatoes, vinegar and sugar and bring to the boil. Turn the heat down to a simmer and cook gently for 20 minutes, until thick. You have to stir it quite a lot or it will stick to the bottom.

Take it off the heat, cover with a lid and leave it to sit while you…

* Tip

The relish makes more than you need but you can freeze it, or it will keep for a few days in the fridge – good in sandwiches.

The Best-ever Beef Burger

To serve

16 rashers of bacon, cooked until crispy (see page 46 if you're in any doubt)

8 slices of Monterey Jack cheese

8 burger buns

150ml mayonnaise

1 cos lettuce

8 large gherkins

Cook the burgers

Either get the barbecue good and hot with the coals glowing or heat a griddle pan over a medium heat (you don't need to add any oil). Place the burgers on the barbecue or griddle and leave for a few minutes until the edges start to colour, then slide a fish slice under each burger and turn over (if they stick, they're not ready to be turned). Leave to cook for a couple of minutes until crisp on the edges, then turn again. It will be about 6 minutes in total. Your burger is now medium. If you want it well done, slide the burgers to a place on the grill where it is slightly cooler or if you are using a griddle pan, reduce the heat. Leave the burgers to cook for a few minutes more.

Now for the toppings

When the burgers are cooked, top with some crispy bacon, then a slice of cheese and leave over the heat until the cheese just starts to melt.

Meanwhile, cut the buns in half, toast them and spread them with mayo. Slide the burger patty on to the bottom of the bun, spoon on a good amount of relish and put the lid on. Serve with the lettuce and gherkins on the side.

Chinese Beer-can Chicken

Beer-can chicken or chook is nothing new. It's clever because the beer boils and steams the chicken from the inside while the chicken is being roasted on the outside. You can cook this either in a barbecue with a lid or in a conventional oven at a very high temperature. My additions to this 'classic' are the Chinese aromatics and a good coating of teriyaki on the outside of the chicken. Enjoy.

Feeds 4–6

100g fresh root ginger, sliced but unpeeled

2 spring onions, chopped

1 garlic clove, crushed

2 teaspoons Chinese five-spice powder

2 teaspoons sugar

1 teaspoon salt

4 star anise

1 large chicken, about 1.5kg

200ml teriyaki sauce*

1 x 375ml can beer

To serve

small bunch of coriander, leaves picked

2 spring onions, cut on the bias

flatbreads, maybe

Hoisin sauce, if you like

In a small bowl, mix together the ginger, spring onions, garlic, Chinese five-spice powder, sugar, salt and star anise. Stuff the cavity of the chicken with the spice mixture and then carefully shake the chicken.

Brush the outside of the chicken all over with teriyaki sauce. You can do all this the night before.

Light the barbecue and let it burn down to embers, or heat the oven to 200°C/gas 6.

Open the can of beer and drink about half of it. Sit the chicken on the can of beer then slide the can inside the chicken so that the can fits snuggly inside the cavity with all the aromatics. Stand the can, balancing the chicken, on a small baking tray.

Put the chicken on the barbecue, close the lid and cook for 40–50 minutes, checking it every so often to make sure the chicken doesn't burn – you may have to regulate the barbecue's temperature but you need to ensure it is hot enough for the beer to boil. If cooking in the oven, cook for 1 hour – don't open the oven door. To check if the chicken is cooked, stab a thigh with a knife or skewer – if the juices run clear the chicken is done. Take it out and let it rest for 15 minutes.

You'll be eating soon. Prize the meat off the chicken and chop it up. Discard the carcase. Scatter over the coriander and spring onions. Good with flatbreads and Hoisin sauce.

* Tip

If you want to make your own teriyaki sauce, put 100ml each of soy sauce, mirin and sake and 30g caster sugar in a pan and boil until only 200ml liquid remains.

Thai Prawn Skewers with Coconut Dressing

I grew up in a world full of prawns and oysters. The latter I did not appreciate until a lot later in life but prawns I have always loved. They should be big, they should be fresh, they should be in their shells and you should have to peel them. Those beauties have the flavour; search them out and pay that little bit extra for them.

I use tamarind water, which is a souring agent, in this recipe. If you can't get hold of it use lime juice but only at the very end. Tamarind can be cooked; lime juice can't as it goes bitter.

For up to 8

24 large prawns, tails peeled and heads on

1 tablespoon light soy sauce

1 tablespoon sesame oil

For the coconut dressing

25ml coconut cream

1 tablespoon Thai red curry paste (bought or my recipe on page 102)

1 teaspoon fish sauce

1 tablespoon palm sugar (or soft brown sugar)

60ml tamarind water (if you can't find it – add lime juice at the end of the recipe)

100ml coconut milk

You will need 12 wooden skewers

Marinate the prawns in the soy sauce and sesame oil for up to an hour. Soak 12 wooden skewers in cold water.

Thread the prawns onto skewers (two prawns per skewer) and place in the fridge.

In a small pan, melt the coconut cream with the curry paste and cook it over a low heat for 2 minutes or until fragrant. Add the fish sauce, palm sugar, tamarind water, if using. Stir well and cook for 1 minute, then add the coconut milk, bring to the boil and simmer for 5 minutes.

In the meantime, light a barbecue or heat a griddle pan. Once the barbecue or griddle is hot, cook the prawns for a couple of minutes on each side (and no more) until the heads go lovely and pink and the tails have a little colour.

Stick the skewers in a bowl, dribble over lots of coconut dressing and serve extra dressing on the side.

My Satay with Peanut Sauce

The main vegetable market in Bangkok is Pak Khlong Talat, which opens at 4am. Street sellers set up to provide the traders and customers with breakfast and this was one of my favourites as I wandered around the stalls. The hawkers place the satay on a glowing hot grill and cook them quickly, fanning the coals for maximum heat but no flame.

For 6

100ml light soy sauce

200ml mirin

100g miso paste

300g chicken, cut into thin strips 3–4cm long, 1cm wide and 0.5cm thick

300g beef steak, cut into thin strips about 4cm long, 1cm wide and 0.5cm thick

300g raw prawns, peeled but with tails left on

For the peanut sauce

50ml vegetable oil

1 shallot, diced

1 tablespoon Thai red curry paste

1 small red chilli, de-seeded and finely chopped

300g crunchy peanut butter

200ml water

50ml soy sauce

You will need 24 wooden skewers

Prep the chicken, beef and prawns

Light the barbecue or heat a griddle pan. Soak 24 wooden skewers in plenty of cold water.

Meanwhile, in a large bowl, mix together the light soy sauce, mirin and miso paste, then divide the mixture among three bowls. Stir the strips of chicken into one, the beef into another and the prawns into the third. Leave to marinate for a few minutes or up to an hour, to allow the meat to absorb some of the flavour.

Make the peanut sauce

Heat the oil in a saucepan over a high heat. Add the shallots and gently fry for a couple of minutes. Add the red curry paste and chilli and cook, stirring all the time, for another couple of minutes or until the paste is fragrant. Stir in the peanut butter and the water and stir well. Bring to the boil, then add the soy sauce and stir again. Bring it back to the boil, then take it straight off the heat.

Cook the satay

Thread two pieces of meat, chicken or prawn onto each wooden skewer – the meat should look long and squiggly. Place the skewers on the barbecue over the glowing coals or on the smoking hot griddle. Turn the skewers over every 30 seconds until the meat and chicken are rich and dark in colour and the prawns have turned pink. Brush with the extra marinade as you cook – they should only take a couple of minutes to cook.

Pile your plates high and have the peanut sauce on the side.

Sausage Rolls of all Kinds

I've been a big fan of sausage rolls from an early age. I don't know what got me hooked but I am – sort of addicted, really. My trick so the sausage rolls are plump and moist is to add water to the sausage meat. This works because it creates steam inside the pastry, making it puff up and stay that way when it's cooked.

I've given you two options for filling the rolls: a classic sausage meat filling and a vego filling made with spinach and ricotta. The spinach and ricotta version needs lots of salt and pepper because ricotta doesn't have a huge amount of flavour, while the egg yolk and flour helps to bind the filling so that it doesn't all just melt away when the rolls are baked. Choose whichever filling you prefer or double the quantity of pastry and make both options.

Makes 12 decent-sized sausage rolls*

vegetable oil, for greasing

450g puff pastry, rolled to 1cm thick (double the quantity if you are making both fillings)

1 egg, beaten, for glazing

plain flour, for dusting

For the sausage meat filling

1 garlic clove, grated

100ml cold water

1kg sausagemeat

salt and freshly ground black pepper

For the spinach and ricotta filling

25g butter

pinch of nutmeg (optional)

350g spinach

500g ricotta cheese

2 egg yolks

30g plain flour

* or 8 massive ones

Heat the oven to 200°C/gas 6. Line a baking sheet with greaseproof paper and rub it with the tiniest amount of vegetable oil.

Make the sausage meat filling

Mix the garlic with the water and a pinch of salt. Put the sausagemeat into a large bowl, pour over the garlic-flavoured water and beat it with a wooden spoon until all the water is mixed in.

Make the rolls

Lay the pastry on a lightly floured worktop. Cut it in half lengthways. Spoon the filling into a plastic piping bag – just fill it halfway or the filling will all come out of the top. Cut the end off the bag so that the nozzle is the thickness of a sausage. Pipe the mixture down the length of one long side of the pastry in one continuous line. Roll the pastry up around the filling, brushing the edges with water to seal. Repeat with the other half of the pastry and filling mixture.

Brush each of the long logs of pastry with the beaten egg. Using a sharp knife, cut the logs into rolls of whatever length you like and arrange on the baking sheet, leaving a good amount of space between each one so they don't touch and they can puff up. Bake for 25–30 minutes, until golden; they will smell cooked, like the smell of a bakery. Take them out of the oven and eat – hot, cold, with tomato sauce. Beware: you may become addicted just like me!

Go posh...

Sprinkle the tops of the sausage rolls with some sesame or poppy seeds after brushing with the beaten egg.

Try adding extra flavourings to the sausagemeat filling: little bits of dried apple, some allspice and coriander or chopped ham.

Sausage Rolls of all Kinds

To make the spinach and ricotta filling

Take a large frying pan. Over a low heat, melt the butter, add salt, pepper and the nutmeg. Wash the spinach then drop the wet spinach into the pan and cook for 2 minutes, then drain the spinach and squeeze it to remove as much extra liquid as possible. Spread it out on a tray and leave to cool.

In a large bowl, mix together the ricotta, egg yolks and flour and a good grind of pepper. Add the spinach, mix well, taste and season again if necessary. Spoon the filling into a plastic piping bag and do the same as for the sausage rolls.

Tip

These pastry wonders can be made way in advance and then frozen, ready to go straight into the oven when you need them. They can be cooked from frozen, just drop the oven temperature by 10 degrees and cook them for an extra 15 minutes. Don't overcrowd the oven – cook in two batches if necessary or the bottoms go soggy, and no one likes a soggy bottom.

Lamb Rumps with Spiced Yoghurt

Anyone who worked the grill section of Quaglino's between 1993 and 1995 will recognise the inspiration for this dish. We would marinate whole boned legs of lamb, 60 at a time, in huge tubs and then, once marinated, we would thread the big nuts of tenderised lamb onto huge skewers that fitted in the massive rotisseries. The result was delicious: spiced, sweet and tender lamb with little bits of charred yoghurt. This is the version I do at home.

Feeds 6–8

juice of 2 lemons, plus extra to finish

small bunch of thyme, leaves stripped

4 rumps of lamb, about 250–300g each

1 teaspoon ground cinnamon

1 teaspoon ground cardamom

1 teaspoon ground turmeric

pinch of cloves

250ml thick yoghurt

2 red chillies, de-seeded and diced

2 garlic cloves, grated

1 lemon

salt and freshly ground black pepper

To marinate the lamb, mix the lemon juice, 1 tablespoon salt and the thyme leaves. Score the lamb fat. Rub the mixture all over the lamb and leave for an hour at room temperature.

Put the spices in a dry frying pan and toast over a medium heat, until fragrant and dark in colour, almost smoking.

Put the yoghurt, chillies, garlic and toasted spices in a bowl and mix to make a paste. Rub the paste all over the lamb and leave to marinate for an hour at room temperature.

Light the barbecue or heat a griddle pan. Once the barbecue has glowing coals or the griddle is smoking hot, cook the lamb, fat-side down, for about 30 minutes, turning every couple of minutes, and continually basting it with the yoghurt paste. Take it off the heat, let it rest for a good 10 minutes. Finish with a squeeze of lemon juice and serve it up.

Serve

As you will – grilled tomatoes, dressed watercress, flatbreads etc.

Paprika Pork

For me, a barbie wouldn't be a barbie without a good pork chop. I love them. However, the recipe for these wonderful hunks of meat can be cooked over coals, in a frying pan or on a griddle. Serve them with a big bunch of peppery watercress. The chutney is sharp and sweet and savoury all at the same time and it works wonders with all grilled meats. So this is a recipe within a recipe; make them together or apart – it's up to you.

For 4

For the tomato chutney

500g ripe tomatoes

1 large onion, diced

½ teaspoon ground ginger

½ teaspoon ground mace

2 garlic cloves, sliced

50g soft dark brown sugar

50ml cider vinegar

½ teaspoon chilli powder

½ teaspoon smoked paprika

good pinch of dried oregano

2 teaspoons plain flour mixed with a little white vinegar to form a smooth paste, for thickening

For the pork

4 good-sized pork loin chops, about 275–350g each, skin on and with a good covering of fat

50ml olive oil

1 teaspoon smoked paprika

½ tablespoon harissa

salt

Get the chutney going and light the barbie

If you're using the barbecue, light it now. Skin the tomatoes. Put them into a bowl and pour over some boiling water so they are covered. Leave them for a few minutes. Drain and let them sit until they're cool. Carefully peel off and discard the skins.

Chop the tomatoes into thumbnail-sized chunks and put them into a large heavy-based pan with the rest of the chutney ingredients, except for the thickening paste. Bring to the boil then turn the heat down and simmer gently for 30 minutes.

Cook the pork

Heat a griddle pan until smoking, or by now your barbecue coals should be just glowing.

Using a sharp knife, score the skin of the pork chops in a criss-cross pattern – the skin cooks better like this.

Mix together the olive oil, paprika, harissa and a little salt in a small bowl and then rub it all over the chops. Gently cook the chops, moving them continuously so they colour but don't blacken and turning them every 2 or 3 minutes – they'll take about 15 minutes to cook through. When they're firm to the touch and the fat has changed colour, take them off the heat and let them rest for 10 minutes.

Finish the chutney

Stir the thickening paste into the thickened chutney, return to the boil and then cook for a further 5 minutes, until thick and sticky.

Serve the chops with salad and the chutney.

Whole Sea Bass with Fennel and Olives

Salt crusting is a bit of an art; it protects the delicate flesh of this much-prized fish and seasons it at the same time. You must use a good-sized sea bass and pack it full of sweet fennel and salty olives. Bake it and let all your friends gasp as you carry it to the table where you should crack the crust. Neptune himself will be patting you on the back for this one.

Feeds 6

1 large sea bass, weighing 2–2.5kg, cleaned and scaled

a little vegetable oil

50ml sherry

50ml olive oil, plus extra for drizzling

1 small bulb of fennel, thinly sliced

2 spring onions, thinly sliced

2 large Serrano chillies, thinly sliced

50g large pitted black olives

800g sea salt

6 egg whites

400g plain flour

200ml water

Heat the oven to 200°C/gas 6.

Wipe out the inside of the fish with kitchen paper so that it is really clean. Rub the outside of the fish all over with a little vegetable oil.

In a large bowl, mix the sherry and olive oil. Add the fennel, spring onions, chillies and olives and mix it all together.

Open the fish and pack the cavity with as much of the fennel mixture as possible – any leftover can be used as a salad to serve with it. Press the opening of the fish closed so that the stuffing stays inside or skewer it if you wish.

Mix the salt with the egg whites, using a fork. Add the flour and mix it all together. Add the water and mix just a little – the mixture should be crumbly. Line a large baking sheet with greaseproof paper, then spread a good layer of the salt paste onto the paper, making it rise on one side so that the fish can lie at an angle and the filling won't run out. Place the fish on top of the salt, then cover the fish with the remaining salt paste, making sure you don't leave any gaps.

Place the fish in the oven and bake for 40 minutes, then remove and leave it to rest for 15 minutes so that the fish relaxes before it's served.

Slide the fish onto a serving plate or a board. Crack open the crust and the fish will appear. Yum. Discard the salt crust, remove the filling from the fish and mix with any reserved filling. Serve it in a bowl alongside the fish. Let everyone dive in and peel away hunks of soft, white delicious fish – turn the page to see how it's done.

Or try...

For an Asian flavour, change the filling from olives etc. to ginger, spring onions and a little sesame oil.

Ribs and Wings

I was taught to cook great spare ribs by a Taiwanese chef who worked with me years ago. The trick is to cook the pork first and then finish it over the coals. The meat is beautifully moist inside, the edges go all crispy and crunchy and the marinade gives it all guts. Both the ribs and the wings only take 20–25 minutes. You could also cook chicken legs and thighs in the same way.

Feeds 8–10

2kg pork belly spare ribs, cut a good 2.5cm thick

200ml oyster sauce

200ml soy sauce

200g soft brown sugar

200ml sherry or Chinese Shaoxing rice wine

100g hunk of fresh root ginger

2 garlic cloves

4 star anise (optional)

1 cinnamon stick

12 chicken wings

Place all the ingredients except the chicken wings in a large pan, cover with water and give everything a good stir – the meat should be free and able to move about; if the meat is packed too tightly you need to use a bigger pan. Put the pan on the hob and bring to the boil, then reduce the heat until the liquid is simmering, give it another stir and cook gently for 1 hour.

Take off the heat and ladle a good amount of the hot liquid over the chicken wings. Leave both the wings and ribs to settle for a good 30 minutes.

Light the barbecue or heat the oven to 220°C/gas 7. Pour off half the chicken cooking liquid and bubble it in a separate pan until it's thick and sticky.

By now the barbecue should be embers or your oven should be hot. Take the ribs and chicken out of the marinade. If you're cooking them in the oven, place them on a tray, cook them for 15 minutes, then brush them with the thick sauce you've made, and give them a stir. Cook them for another 10 minutes – they should go all crispy and dark.

If you're using the barbecue, put the ribs and wings on the grill and brush them with the sauce. Cook for 5 minutes, turn them, brush them with more sauce, cook them for another 5 minutes, turn them again, brush them with more sauce and cook for 5 minutes. Turn them, brush them with more sauce, then cook for a final 5 minutes.

Put the ribs and wings in a big bowl. Have plenty of fingers bowls and maybe some napkins, and let everybody dig in*.

* Turn over to see what happens next…

Roast Pumpkin and Charred Onion Salad

Sweet, bitter and a little salty, that's what I think makes this salad a bit different. It may sound autumnal but it can be served warm or cold all year round with the squashes that are in season. Make it posh or not – serve it up in a big bowl or be creative and make a pretty plate of it.

Feeds 4–6

30ml olive oil, with extra for drizzling

4 small onions, halved through their middle (like through their equator)

500g piece of pumpkin or butternut squash, peeled, de-seeded and cut into golfball-sized chunks

100g curd cheese

a small handful of flat-leaf parsley, leaves picked

salt and freshly ground black pepper

Heat the oven to 220°C/gas 7.

Rub a large ovenproof frying pan with a little bit of oil (an ovenproof one saves on washing up). Put the onions, cut-side down, into the pan and fry over a high heat for a good 5 minutes, without moving them, until coloured.

In a large bowl, toss the pumpkin with the remaining oil and season with salt and pepper. Add to the pan of onions. Now you can move the onions. Give the pan a good shake so the onions come free and the pumpkin is mixed in. Put the pan into the oven and roast for 25 minutes, until the pumpkin is golden and dark on the outside.

Take the pan out of the oven, pour the veg into a serving bowl, dot the curd cheese over the vegetables in splodges, season with black pepper and salt, drizzle with olive oil and toss the parsley over the top. Done.

Some things just take time. So enjoy the preparation, leave these beauties overnight and the rewards will be tenfold.

leave
overnight

Five-hour Roast Pork Belly

This is one of my signature dishes and it has appeared on menus far and wide. Over the years, I reckon it has satisfied some half a million people. Seriously.

It is also quite simply a crowd-pleaser and something I love to cook at home. Yes, you have to start it the day before but it really is the easiest of recipes.

For 10–12 very hungry people, with leftovers

For the pork

3.5–4kg piece of pork belly, bone in, skin on

2 tablespoons salt

8 garlic cloves, smashed with the back of a knife

4 tablespoons smoked paprika

60ml vegetable oil

2 lemons, halved lengthways then thickly sliced

4 large potatoes, peeled and halved

And don't forget the ingredients for the mash and salsa verde which are on the next page...

Day 1: marinate the pork

Using a very sharp knife (I use a Stanley knife), score the skin of the pork really deeply in a criss-cross pattern with about a 1cm gap between each cut. Boil your kettle, put the pork in a clean sink, skin-side up, and pour the boiling water over the skin of the pork – this scalds it and it will make sure the skin is crispy once it is roasted.

Take a large bowl and mix the salt, garlic, paprika, vegetable oil and lemon pieces. Now, rub the mixture into the pork skin and flesh, and leave the lemon pieces sitting on top of the skin. Put the pork into a tray and leave it to marinate in the fridge for 12–24 hours.

Day 2: roast the pork (this is going to take 5 hours!)

Heat the oven to 160°C/gas 3.

Put the potatoes for the pork into a roasting tin – the potatoes will act as a trivet. Lay the pork, skin-side up, on top of the potatoes and pour over any marinade left in the tray. Pour a large cup of water into the bottom of the tray underneath the pork.

Cover the pork with greaseproof paper, then with foil and tuck the foil around the outside of the tin to seal it. It's now going to cook nicely for 4 hours.

Take the pork out of the oven, turn the oven temperature up to 200°C/gas 6 and carefully remove the foil – the tin will be steaming. Put the pork back in the oven and roast for a further hour.

Still not done, I'm sorry to say. Take the delicious pork out of the oven and leave it to sit somewhere warm to rest for 30 minutes. While the pork is resting, make the mashed potato and the salsa verde.

Continued...

Five-hour Roast Pork Belly

...from the previous page

For the mash

2kg potatoes, peeled and cut into chunks about the size of a golf ball

200ml milk, plus extra if necessary

50ml double cream

70g butter, plus extra if necessary

salt and white pepper

For the salsa verde

2 large handfuls of flat-leaf parsley, leaves picked

a large handful of basil, leaves picked

2 garlic cloves

1 boiled egg

a handful of fresh white breadcrumbs

1 tablespoon white vinegar

1 tablespoon capers

50ml olive oil

pinch of salt

Make the mash

Put the spuds into a large pan, cover with cold water and add 2 teaspoons of salt. Bring to the boil and simmer for about 20 minutes, until tender. Drain well, shaking off all the excess water, then put them back in the pan (off the heat), cover with a tea towel and leave for 5 minutes.

Mash the potatoes with a fork – a fork doesn't squash the spuds like a masher would. Put the pan on a low heat, add the milk, cream and butter and mix well. Add salt and white pepper – lots if you're me.

For the salsa verde

Put the parsley, basil and garlic into a food processor and pulse until chunky. Add all the rest of the ingredients and pulse for 30 seconds or until the mixture has a roughly chopped texture – it should not be a paste.

Almost there...

Now the pork has rested, lift it out of the tin and lay it skin-side down on a board. Score the underside of the pork so that you can see the ends of the bones. Pop them out with your thumb, then take the bones out by simply pulling at the sticking out ends – they should pull away from the flesh easily. Cut the pork in half lengthways, then cut each half into five or six slices. Flip each one over– it should be a lovely glistening slice of roasted deliciousness. The whole board goes to the table. Bowls of mash, bowls of salsa verde – go for it!

NB

The potatoes left in the bottom of the tin are delicious but carry a health warning.

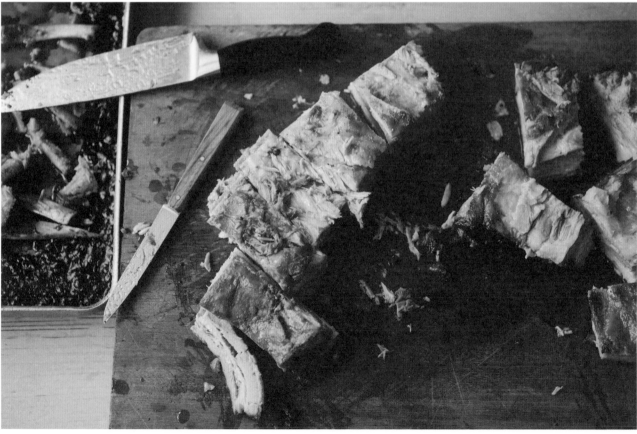

Gnudi with Beef Ragout

I am fortunate to travel a lot but I am always looking for new ideas and interesting produce. It was on a trip through Italy that I first tasted gnudi (as in rudie nudie) – little balls of soft ricotta cheese coated in a semolina shell. I ate an amazing lunch in a tiny roadside café where these little dumplings were served with butter and sage; they blew my mind. The secret is to leave the soft ricotta covered in semolina overnight so that it forms a casing around the cheese. When they are boiled the semolina becomes like a pasta shell and keeps the ricotta inside. So clever. This is my version, and it's a recipe within a recipe, as the gnudi and the ragout can be made separately, but together they are divine.

Feeds 8-10

For the gnudi

500g ricotta

100g Parmesan, finely grated, plus extra to serve

1 good teaspoon freshly ground black pepper

500g fine semolina flour

For the beef ragout

2kg beef shin and/or beef skirt or ox cheek, cut into credit-card sized chunks

2 carrots, peeled

2 leeks, split and washed

2 celery sticks

small bunch of sage

2 bay leaves

100ml vegetable oil

200g thick bacon, cut into big chunks

2 x 400g tins chopped tomatoes

1 bottle of red wine

a big handful of chopped flat-leaf parsley

salt and freshly ground black pepper

The first day, make the gnudi

In a large bowl, mash the ricotta with a fork and then mix in the Parmesan and the black pepper. Divide into four balls, then divide each ball into eight and roll again.

Spread a little of the semolina flour on a plate and coat each gnudi in semolina. Spread half the remaining semolina across a flat tray or baking sheet. Place the gnudi on the tray, spacing them out so that they do not touch each other, and pour the rest of the semolina over the top so that the gnudi are almost completely covered. Leave in the fridge, very loosely covered in cling film, for 24 hours.

The next day, make the beef ragout

Heat the oven to 190°C/gas 5. Season the meat really well with salt and pepper. Tightly tie the carrots, leeks, celery, sage and bay leaves in a bundle with cooking string.

Heat the oil in a large casserole, add the bacon and cook over a high heat for 4–5 minutes, until crispy. Take it out and put it to one side. Add the meat and leave it to sit and sizzle for a good 5 minutes, until the chunks are well browned underneath and naturally come away from the pan. Turn the meat over and cook for a further 5 minutes or until browned on the other side.

Add the bundle of vegetables and herbs, the cooked bacon, the tomatoes and wine, bring to the boil and let the sauce bubble away for about 10 minutes, scraping the sticky bits of meat from the bottom of the pot with a wooden spoon. Now pour in a litre or so of water so that the liquid almost covers the meat. Cover the casserole with a lid and put it into the oven to cook for 1 hour.

Gnudi with Beef Ragout

Take the casserole out, give the ragout a good stir and then pop it back in the oven, uncovered, for another hour. The liquid will evaporate and the top will become all crusty and beefy and stewy. Take it out of the oven and leave it to cool, uncovered, for 30 minutes or so.

Take the hunks of meat out and put them in a bowl. Take the bundle of veg out and put it on a chopping board. Cut off the string and throw it away. Also discard the bay leaves and the sage. Chop the veg into chunks and drop them back into the sauce. Put the sauce back on the heat and bring it to the boil – it should be soupy rather than thick.

Now use two forks to pull the meat apart from the centre and then shred it. Toss the shredded meat back into the sauce. Turn off the heat and put a lid on it.

Cook the gnudi

Bring a large pan of salted water to the boil. Dust any excess semolina off the gnudi and drop half of them into the boiling water. Wait until they float to the surface, then let them cook gently for 3 minutes. If they boil ferociously they'll bump into each other and break. Lift the gnudi out with a slotted spoon and drop them straight into the stew. Cook the other half.

Stir the gnudi and the ragout together, then sprinkle a good handful of parsley over the top. Spoon into bowls and serve with a big hunk of Parmesan and a grater.

Cassoulet with Salt Pork and White Beans

As much as I would love to say that there is a quick way of cooking this dish, there really isn't. However, it is a great big pot of porky, beany brilliance. So do as I do and take it on as a two-day project. Enjoy the time it takes to shop and soak and salt and boil. This is a feast and it will feed a horde of merry men and women. Serve as a big pot or in pretty little bowls; even the most butch pot can be made to look beautiful. This is so tasty and with all the time spent making it I feel it deserves to be made to look luxurious.

Feeds 10–12 merry people

600g boneless pork belly

100g salt

500g dried haricot beans

1 knuckle of smoked ham hock, bone in (about 500g in weight)

3 thick slices of bacon (not rashers), skin on

6 litres water

50ml olive oil, plus a little extra for frying

2 sprigs of thyme

3 carrots, peeled and cut into chunks

1 large onion, peeled and stuck with 4 cloves

2kg tomatoes, chopped

1 Morteau sausage

4 Toulouse sausages

For the green breadcrumbs

100g fresh fine white breadcrumbs

1 garlic clove, crushed

40g flat-leaf parsley, finely chopped

1 tablespoon olive oil

salt and freshly ground black pepper

The night before you want to serve...

Rub the pork belly all over with the salt and place on a tray. Leave it in the fridge. Put the beans, ham knuckle and bacon into a large casserole and pour over 5 litres of the water. Leave to soak overnight in your fridge, or somewhere cool if it won't fit.

The next day: roast the pork and start the cassoulet

Heat the oven to 160°C/gas 3.

Wipe the salt off the pork belly and then rub it with a wet cloth. Now rub it with the olive oil. Put the pork belly, skin-side up on a trivet in a roasting tin and roast in the oven for 2 hours.

Strain the soaked beans, ham knuckle and bacon. Give the casserole a good rinse, and return the beans, knuckle and bacon to the pot, adding the thyme, carrots, onion, tomatoes and the remaining litre of water as well. Bring the whole lot to the boil and simmer for a good 5 minutes. Cover with a lid, then put it in the oven (alongside the pork belly) for 45 minutes. Take the lid off and cook for another hour, at least, or until the beans are tender and are just about to split.

While that's cooking you need to make the breadcrumbs and cook the sausages.

Make the breadcrumbs

Put the breadcrumbs, garlic, parsley, olive oil, and a good pinch of salt and a grind of pepper into a food processor. Blitz for 1 minute and you'll have lovely green breadcrumbs.

Continued...

Cassoulet with Salt Pork and White Beans

...from the previous page

Cook the sausages

Lower the Morteau sausage into a pan of boiling water and simmer for 30 minutes. Heat a teaspoon of olive oil or so in a frying pan and fry the Toulouse sausages over a medium heat, until browned all over. Put them both on a tray and cover with foil.

Take the pork belly out of the oven and leave it to cool. Put it on a chopping board, slice it into long strips, then into cubes.

Take the casserole out of the oven and put the ham knuckle and bacon on a board. Take out the onion, discard the cloves, and roughly chop up the onion. Using a sharp knife, cut the skin off the ham knuckle and discard it, then use two forks to pull the meat apart into chunks about the size of your thumb. Chop the bacon into lardons. Add the pulled meat and the bacon to the beans and give everything a really good stir to break up the tomatoes. You now have a big pot of pork and bean stew – or, a cassoulet.

Cut the Toulouse sausages in half. Slice the Morteau sausage.

Almost there...

Here you've got two choices: classically, for a hearty meal you mix all the meat into the beans. Cover it with the breadcrumbs and bake it for another 20 minutes or until the breadcrumbs have browned.

Or, like me, toast the breadcrumbs in a frying pan until they turn golden, spoon out pretty little bowls of cassoulet, top with pieces of the meat, and sprinkle with the toasted breadcrumbs.

I love mine with loads of mustard and a large bottle of red wine.

I love a good dessert – a proper steaming pudding with thick custard or real ice cream. So here are cakes, tarts, pies and puds, and lots of them.

and to finish

Sticky Orange Polenta Cake

Over the centuries, many culinary inventions have been inspired by the scarcity of basic ingredients, such as flour and eggs. Necessity is the mother of invention...This cake is definitely one of those creations. Who would have thought that whole oranges and olive oil could make such a grand cake? Sweet, sticky and addictive, the cake has a shelf life of at least a week if you keep it in an airtight tin. Serve it either hot or cold.

Makes 1 cake

2 Seville oranges

2 lemons

180g blanched almonds

4 eggs

big pinch of salt

170g caster sugar

80ml olive oil, plus extra for greasing

150g polenta

10g baking powder

For the syrup

juice of 2–3 Seville oranges (about 150ml)

75g caster sugar

Heat the oven to 180°C/gas 4. Grease a 23cm springform cake tin.

Put 1 orange and 1 lemon into a large pan, cover with water, and place a circle of greaseproof paper over the top so the fruit sits under the water. Bring to the boil, then reduce the heat and simmer for about 30 minutes. Take off the heat.

Toast the blanched almonds in a dry frying pan. Put them in a food processor and blitz until finely ground.

Take the cooked orange and lemon out of the pan. Cut them in half and pick out the seeds. Juice the other fresh orange and lemon (throw away the shells). Put the cooked fruit (skins and all) and extra freshly squeezed juice in the food processor and blend to make a paste.

In a large bowl, beat the eggs with the salt until foaming. Add the sugar and beat again, then add the orange paste, almonds and olive oil. Beat again.

In a separate bowl, mix the polenta and baking powder, then gently fold this into the orange mixture until it is all mixed together.

Pour the mixture into the greased tin and bake for 50 minutes or until a skewer inserted into the centre comes out clean.

Meanwhile, make the syrup. Put the orange juice and sugar in a pan and simmer over a low heat until you have a glossy syrup.

Turn the cake out of the tin onto a serving plate and pour the syrup over it while it's warm.

Tip

If you wrap up the cake (without its syrup) in a sheet of greaseproof paper and a clean tea towel it will stay moist, become stickier and last for about a week.

Lime and Ginger Granita

This dessert is delicious because the icy granita is infused with the warmth of ginger and the sharpness of lime. Pour over some vodka, add a little fresh mint and wait for the sun to set and the party to begin.

175g caster sugar

1 vanilla pod, split lengthways and seeds scraped out

50g fresh root ginger, peeled and crushed so its juice is running

400ml boiling water

60ml lime juice, plus the grated zest of 2 limes to serve

40ml milk

First, make a sugar syrup. Put the sugar, vanilla pod and seeds, ginger and the boiling water into a pan, bring to the boil and boil until the sugar dissolves and both the vanilla and the ginger flavour the syrup – you should be able to smell them. Strain into a large bowl and leave to cool.

Mix the lime juice into the syrup, then add the milk and stir again. Pour the syrup into a plastic container and freeze for 3 hours.

Take the container out of the freezer and use a fork to break up the ice crystals. Put it back in the freezer for a few more hours, then run a fork through it again.

Serve. I like mine served with a sprinkling of lime zest over the top. You can store the granita in the freezer for a few days but always give it a good stir with a fork before you serve so it's fluffy.

Good with...

Some raspberries, on top of poached peaches or in little pots with some chopped pineapple.

Berry and Mascarpone Tarts

These simple little tarts are just a joy. Buttery and sweet and soft and comforting – what more could you want? The key to their success is the combination of sharp yet sweet fruit and a whipped cream filling, and not being too precious about how they look. The pastry can be a bit wonky but the soft fruit is so pretty it doesn't matter.

Makes 12

For the pastry

500g plain flour, plus extra for dusting

pinch of salt

250g softened butter, cubed

150g icing sugar, sifted

4 egg yolks

50ml water

For the filling

300g mascarpone

120ml double cream

50g caster sugar

1 vanilla pod, slit lengthways and seeds scraped out

2 small punnets of berries (raspberries and blackberries – or whatever is in season), washed

1 x 200g tin cherries in syrup, drained

You will need one 12-hole jam tart tins and a fluted cutter

Heat the oven to 200°C/gas 6.

Make the pastry

Sift the flour and salt onto a worktop. Make a well in the centre, add the butter and icing sugar and gently work them together with your fingertips. Add the egg yolks and gradually draw in the flour, adding drops of the water as you go, until a dough forms. Shape the dough into a ball, wrap in cling film and chill in the fridge for at least 20 minutes.

On a lightly floured worktop, roll out the pastry and use a fluted cutter to cut out circles large enough to line the cups of a 12-hole jam tart tin (the cutter should be just a bit bigger than the size of a hole – normally about 6cm). Bake in the oven for 10–12 minutes – they'll puff up in the centre. Take the tin out of the oven and push the centre down with a piece of baking paper, then put them back in the oven and bake for a further 5 minutes to cook the pastry completely. Turn the pastry cases out of their tins onto a wire rack and leave to cool.

Fill and top the tarts

Beat the mascarpone with the cream, sugar and vanilla seeds until fluffy.

Spoon some of the filling into each tart and top with berries and cherries.

Chocolate and Coconut Pie

This is one of those Australianisms that probably started life as a banoffee pie or maybe a lemon meringue pie but developed into a boozy chocolate pie. It's topped with a caramel-flavoured Italian meringue that just needs to be browned with a blowtorch or in the oven.

Enough for 10–12

350g digestive biscuits

120g butter, melted

55g desiccated coconut

200g milk chocolate, broken into pieces

200g dark chocolate, broken into pieces

250ml double cream

180ml milk

100g soft light brown sugar

4 egg yolks (keep the egg whites for the meringue)

150ml coconut liqueur, such as Malibu

40g cornflour

For the meringue

220g caster sugar

60ml water

4 egg whites

½ teaspoon cream of tartar

Make the base

Place the biscuits, melted butter and 25g of the desiccated coconut in a food-processor and blitz until they form crumbs. Press the crumbs into a 23cm fluted tart tin, making sure the crumbs cover the base and come all the way up the sides of the tin. Chill in the fridge.

Make the filling

Slowly heat the chocolates, cream, milk and sugar in a large pan over a low heat, stirring all the time, until the chocolate has melted and you have a thick mixture.

In a large bowl, beat the egg yolks with the coconut liqueur and cornflour. Set the bowl over a pan of gently simmering water (making sure the water doesn't touch the base of the bowl). Pour the hot chocolate mixture into the bowl and give it a good stir. What you're making here is chocolate custard. Keep stirring it for about 5 minutes or until it becomes thick. Take off the heat and leave to cool for 10 minutes, stirring it continuously until it's cool.

Pour the custard into the biscuit case and spread it out evenly. Sprinkle with the remaining desiccated coconut and put it into the fridge to chill for a good hour.

Continues...

Chocolate and Coconut Pie

Make the meringue

Put the sugar and water into a small pan, bring to the boil and continue to boil for about 5 minutes (don't stir it) until the sugar has melted and the mixture becomes a light caramel colour.

Meanwhile, in a large bowl, whisk the egg whites with the cream of tartar until they form stiff peaks (an electric whisk is good for this).

Now it's time to make Italian meringue. Once the caramel has its tan, take it off the heat and leave it to cool for 3 minutes. While beating, slowly drizzle the hot sugar into the egg whites, but you've got to keep on beating. Add all the sugar mixture and continue to beat until the meringue is shiny.

Pie time

Take the set custard base out of the fridge and spoon the meringue over the top. Either heat the oven to 220°/gas 7 or use a blowtorch to brown the top of the meringue. If using the oven, leave it for 3 minutes or until the meringue starts to colour – keep an eye on it.

And it will look like this...

Steamed Passion Fruit and Mango Puddings with Custard

This recipe is my life in a dessert: passion fruit – so Australian – and steamed pudding – so British. I like to make individual puddings as a large pudding cooked in a basin can be a bit heavy and, as you can see, they are as pretty as a picture if you use the moulds. However, you could also use soufflé dishes and serve the puddings without turning them out.

Makes 8

For the passion fruit and mango purée

8 passion fruit, halved, pulp scooped out

1 tablespoon caster sugar

100g mango purée (from a tin)

For the pudding mix

250g butter, plus extra for greasing

250g caster sugar, plus extra for coating the moulds

4 eggs

250g self-raising flour

50ml milk

few drops of vanilla essence

For the custard

300ml milk

2 drops of vanilla essence

3 egg yolks

40g caster sugar

10g plain flour

10g cornflour

Prep the moulds

Heat the oven to 180°C/gas 4. Grease eight little pudding moulds and fill one of the moulds with 20g of sugar, swirl it around the mould to coat the insides, then pour the sugar into the next mould and repeat until all the moulds have a coating of sugar. Discard any excess sugar. Line the bases with baking paper.

Make the purée

Put the passion fruit pulp in a pan with the sugar and mango and bring to the boil. Take it off the heat and strain off half the passion fruit seeds. Put a good tablespoon of the mixture into the base of each prepared mould.

Make the pudding mix

In a large bowl, use an electric hand whisk to beat the butter and sugar until creamy and white. Add the eggs one at a time, beating well after each one, and scraping the sides of the bowl every so often until all the eggs are mixed in.

Add the flour to the butter mixture with the milk and vanilla essence and beat until mixed together and sticky.

Spoon or pipe the pudding mixture into each mould, filling the moulds about two-thirds full. Cover each mould with kitchen foil and wrap tightly.

Put a clean tea towel into the base of a deep roasting tin and cover it with 2cm of warm water (this makes a bain-marie). Place the pudding moulds in the tin, spacing them evenly. Place in the oven and bake for 35 minutes. The filling will be pushing the foil up and the puddings will no longer be wobbly.

Now for the custard...

Steamed Passion Fruit and Mango Puddings with Custard

... from the previous page

Make the custard

Put the milk and vanilla essence in a pan and bring to the boil.
Meanwhile, in a small bowl, beat together the egg yolks and sugar
until white and then beat in the flours. As the milk comes to the boil,
pour it over the egg mixture and beat well. You now have custard.
Pour the custard back into the pan, place over a low heat and
cook for a few minutes, stirring all the time with a wooden spoon
and it will go thick, as custard should be.

Serve

Once the puddings are cooked, let them rest a little and then
remove the foil and turn out each mould onto an individual plate.
Peel off the paper on top. Scrape any excess pulp out of the
moulds and drizzle it over the puddings. Serve with the custard.

Flavours

Try using other fruit pulps, plum or strawberry jam, chocolate and
hazelnut spread or lemon or lime curd.

Gateau St Emilion

Anyone who ever worked or ate at Terence Conran's Le Pont de la Tour restaurant in the shadows of Tower Bridge will recognise this recipe. I started working at Le Pont, as we called it, when I was just 26 and we made this cake daily, ready for the next day's service. When not in whole gateau form, the cake was served in little pots topped with the booziest amaretti biscuits. This is so rich and so delicious and so potent that there is little else to say – enjoy.

For 12, at least

150g amaretti biscuits or macaroons

50ml brandy

120g unsalted butter, softened

120g caster sugar

100ml whole milk

100ml single cream

250g good-quality dark chocolate (70 per cent cocoa solids), broken into bits

3 egg yolks

Line a 20cm loose-bottomed cake tin with cling film so that it comes all the way up the sides and there is a little overhang to lift the gateau out when it's set. Crush 100g of the biscuits, then spread them out over the base of the tin (this will become the top of the gateau). Pour the brandy over the biscuits to soak them.

Put the butter and sugar into a stand mixer fitted with the whisk attachment and beat until white and fluffy.

Meanwhile put the milk and the cream in a small saucepan over a medium heat. As the milk and cream come to the boil whip the pan off the heat and drop in the broken chocolate and the egg yolks and stir until all the chocolate has melted and there are no lumps.

Now, with the mixer on a slow speed, gently start to pour the hot chocolate sauce into the mixer bowl. Mix together very well and leave to beat slowly for 5 minutes until the mixture cools and the chocolate looks more like the consistency of mousse. Pour the moussey chocolate over the soaked biscuits and tap the tin so the mixture sits flat and fills the whole ring.

Crush the remaining biscuits and sprinkle them over the top. Leave the gateau in the fridge for a good 4 hours, or preferably the whole day, to set and become firm. Check it's fully set by pushing your thumb into it; it should leave an imprint. Once firm, invert the gateau onto a plate then lift off the tin. The soaked biscuits will now be on the top. Now peel away the cling film. Serve in thin slices.

My Honeycomb Popcorn with Chocolate Sauce and Ice Cream

Popcorn is good and vanilla ice cream with chocolate sauce is good, so if you put them all together you get something that is brilliant. You can cheat by buying flavoured popcorn but I like to make my own as it's not hard. What I love about this dessert is you can posh it up with a lace tablecloth and a few pretty plates.

Enough for 4

1 tablespoon vegetable oil

120g popping corn kernels

½ teaspoon salt

vanilla ice cream, to serve

For the popcorn coating

90g clear honey

80g caster sugar

50g soft light brown sugar

40g butter

1 teaspoon bicarbonate of soda

For the chocolate sauce

150ml single cream

150g dark chocolate (70 per cent cocoa solids), broken into bits

Make popcorn

Heat the oil in a large pan, which has a well-fitting lid, over a high heat. Add the corn kernels, cover with a lid and cook for 5 minutes, shaking the pan every now and then (don't open it!) – you should hear the corn exploding. Take off the heat and sprinkle with the salt.

Coat it

Put all the coating ingredients, except for the bicarbonate of soda, in a small pan, bring to the boil and cook for 3 minutes or until thick and golden. Turn off the heat. You will need to work quickly now. Add the bicarbonate of soda and stir until the mixture puffs up like honeycomb. Immediately pour the coating over the hot popcorn and mix it through.

Make the sauce

Heat the cream in a small saucepan until it is just about to boil, then whip it off the heat and add the chocolate. Stir with a wooden spoon (don't whisk it or the cream will split) until all the chocolate has melted.

Serve

Put 2 scoops of vanilla ice cream into a large cup or mug, scatter with some popcorn and pour over the hot chocolate sauce.

Ginger Puddings with Caramel Ice Cream

These steamed puddings are one of my all-time favourites. They bring a smile to young and old and as the ending to any meal I know of few things that go down as well. The caramel ice cream demands Jersey cream (that's cream from a Jersey cow not cream from the island of Jersey!) because it has a very high fat content so it freezes without crystals. A cream with less fat will be okay but the ice cream won't be as smooth or as decadent.

Serves 8

For the caramel ice cream

450g caster sugar

625ml cold water

8 egg yolks

1 litre Jersey cream

For the ginger puds

caster sugar, for sprinkling

100g stem ginger in syrup, finely sliced and syrup reserved

160g unsalted butter, plus extra for greasing

130g dark brown sugar

1½ tablespoons molasses

2 eggs, beaten

250g self-raising flour

2 teaspoons ground ginger

½ teaspoon baking powder

a splash of milk

You will need eight 150ml ramekins or dariole moulds

Pudding day minus one: make the ice cream

Put the sugar and 125ml of the water in a large pan over a high heat and bring it to 180°C (use a sugar thermometer). Take off the heat and gradually add 250ml of the water – be very careful, it will bubble up. Put the pan back on the heat and bring it back to the boil. Add the remaining 250ml of water, bring back to the boil again, then remove from the heat and leave the caramel syrup to cool for 5 minutes.

Meanwhile, in a large bowl, use an electric whisk to beat the egg yolks for about 10 minutes, until they're white, thick and almost fill the bowl. Continuing to whisk, slowly add the caramel syrup in a thin stream, pouring it down the sides of the bowl to stop hot syrup flying everywhere. Continue to whisk until cool.

Lightly whip the cream to soft peaks. Fold the whipped cream into the caramel custard and mix thoroughly. Pour the ice cream mixture into a plastic container, seal with a lid and freeze overnight.

On the day...

Ginger Puddings with Caramel Ice Cream

Pud day

Heat the oven to 180°C/gas 4. Grease eight 150ml ramekins or dariole moulds with a little butter and sprinkle with caster sugar. Cut out little circles of baking parchment and put them on the bottom of the moulds.

Arrange the ginger slices in the ramekins or moulds, overlapping them, and drizzle with a little of the reserved syrup to cover the base. Place the ramekins or moulds on a baking sheet.

Beat the butter and dark brown sugar in a large bowl using an electric whisk. Now add the molasses and beat again. Slowly add the eggs and continue to beat for a couple more minutes – it goes thick and dark.

Sift the dry ingredients into a separate bowl. Then pour the dry mixture into the wet sugar mix, adding the splash of milk, and beat until they're mixed together.

Spoon the pudding batter into the ramekins or moulds, so they're three quarters full, and tap the bottom on the worktop so the mixture is even. Cover each one with foil and bake for 30 minutes or until a skewer inserted into the centre of the pudding comes out clean. Take out of the oven and leave to settle for 10–15 minutes.

Almost there...

A few minutes before serving, remove the ice cream from the freezer to allow it to soften slightly.

Using your fingertips, gently press down on the edges of the puddings to bring the sides away from the moulds, or run a knife around the edges, and turn them out onto individual plates. Serve with the ice cream.

Chocolate Ice Cream and Amaretti Biscuit Sandwiches

I didn't really eat ice cream as a kid because I was allergic to it. I know, what a thing to be allergic to! However, every so often I would risk a breathless reaction and have an Eskimo pie – vanilla ice cream sandwiched between biscuits. This recipe is a good cheat because you can buy the biscuits and chocolate ice cream.

Makes as many as you like

1 x 500ml tub good-quality chocolate ice cream

1 x 150g bag crunchy amaretti biscuits

100g almonds, chopped

Take the ice cream out of the freezer a good hour before you want to use it. Put the whole lot in a bowl and beat it with an electric whisk so it goes fluffy. Then put it back in the freezer to set a little.

Spoon some ice cream onto the base of a biscuit and then sandwich the ice cream with another biscuit.

Spread the almonds on a plate and roll the ice cream part of each sandwich in the almonds to coat well. Place the sandwiches on a tray and pop into the freezer for 15 minutes – they should firm up a little.

Go all out...

Make larger sandwiches by replacing the amaretti with digestive or garibaldi biscuits.

Sandwich peanut butter ice cream between Anzac biscuits.

Chocolate Soufflés with Rich Chocolate Sauce

As an apprentice, I made soufflés nearly every day – and lots of them. It was the 1980s and the food revolution in Australia was about to happen so classic French dishes were on all good menus and a soufflé was a must. I discovered that whatever flavour of fresh fruit soufflé I made, nothing sold like a chocolate one. So these chocolate soufflés are little beauties that are easy and really work. They're magic.

Makes 8

45g unsalted butter, softened

30g plain flour

10g unsweetened cocoa powder, plus extra for dusting

225ml milk

1 vanilla pod, split lengthways and seeds scraped out

3 egg yolks

45g dark chocolate (70 per cent cocoa solids), chopped

2 teaspoons rum or liqueur

butter, for greasing

6 egg whites

40g caster sugar

ice cream, to serve

For the rich chocolate sauce

125ml single cream

1 tablespoon caster sugar

60g dark chocolate (70 per cent cocoa solids), chopped

10g butter

You will need eight 150ml soufflé dishes

Make the soufflé base

In a large bowl, beat the butter until smooth, sift in the flour and cocoa powder and beat together.

Put the milk and vanilla pod and seeds in a pan and bring to the boil, then immediately pour the milk over the butter mix. Put the whole lot back in the pan, place it over a medium heat and bring it back to the boil, whisking all the time. As soon as it boils, take it off the heat and whisk in the egg yolks, chopped chocolate and booze. Remove the vanilla pod.

Pour the soufflé base onto a tray or plate, cover the surface with cling film to prevent the mixture forming a skin and leave to cool completely.

Heat the oven to 190°C/gas 5. Generously grease the soufflé dishes and dust with a little cocoa powder to coat the insides, tipping out any excess.

Whip the egg whites

Wipe clean a large bowl. Whisk the egg whites using an electric whisk until soft peaks form. Add half the caster sugar and whisk until the whites form stiff peaks, then add the remaining sugar and whisk for another minute until shiny.

Scrape the cooled soufflé base into a separate bowl and beat it. Add half the egg whites to the soufflé base and gently fold in. When the mixture is evenly mixed, add the rest of the egg whites and fold those through as well – the whole lot should be chocolatey brown.

Almost there...

Chocolate Soufflés with Rich Chocolate Sauce

Cook the soufflés

Spoon the soufflé mixture into the greased dishes, tap the bottom of each one so the mixture flattens, and smooth the surfaces with a palette knife. So that the soufflés will rise evenly, you need to make sure the ramekin is free from any egg white around the top edge. Run your thumb around the top of the mixture to clean the edge of the dish and make a moat around the edge of the soufflé top between ramekin and mixture. Place the ramekins on a baking sheet and put them in the oven. Bake for 15 minutes – DO NOT open the oven door during this time.

Make the chocolate sauce

Put the cream and sugar in a small pan and bring to the boil. Remove from the heat and beat in the chocolate and butter until the chocolate has melted and the sauce is thick and glossy.

Get ready...

As soon as the soufflés are ready, take the baking sheet out of the oven and carry it straight to the table – everyone should be ready to use their napkin to pick up a soufflé and put it on their plate. Serve the soufflés with the chocolate sauce and a scoop of ice cream.

Banana and Chocolate Parfait

Parfaits are soft and luscious – a cross between ice cream and mousse. The Italians call them 'semi freddo', meaning half frozen. This one is particularly delicious because it is made with a great combo of chocolate, banana and nuts. Whipping the egg yolks and cream makes the mixture lighter, which means that the parfait will slice easily once it has been frozen. A parfait will last for a good month in the freezer if it is well wrapped in greaseproof paper and then cling film.

Enough for 8

500ml milk

150ml double cream, plus an extra 150ml, whipped

6 egg yolks

200g caster sugar

100g dark chocolate

1 banana, chopped

For the meringue

100g egg whites

pinch of cream of tartar

50g caster sugar

50g ground hazelnuts

You will need a 1.5-litre loaf tin

Make the parfait

Bring the milk and cream to the boil in a large pan. Meanwhile, beat the egg yolks and sugar together in a large bowl until they have doubled in size – the mix should be all white and fluffy and creamy.

When the milk and cream has come to the boil, stir the egg mixture into it and cook over a low heat for a good 5 minutes, stirring constantly, until it starts to thicken. You're basically making custard. Break the chocolate into a bowl and strain the hot custard over, through a fine sieve. Keep stirring, until the chocolate melts, then fold in the whipped cream and stir in the bananas. Leave to cool.

Line a 1.5-litre loaf tin with cling film. Pour the parfait mixture into the tin and freeze for at least 8 hours.

Make the meringues

Heat the oven to 120°C/gas ½. In a large bowl, whisk the egg whites and the cream of tartar using an electric hand whisk until they form stiff peaks. Add the sugar and whisk until they turn shiny, then fold in the ground hazelnuts.

Spoon the meringue mixture into a piping bag fitted with a 1cm plain nozzle and pipe 15–20cm sticks – they can be a bit rustic – onto a lined baking sheet. Bake for about 1 hour or until crisp. Turn off the oven and leave the meringue to cool in the oven. Any leftovers will keep for 3 days in a sealed biscuit tin.

Dip the parfait tin into a sink of warm water. Turn the parfait out onto a plate or board, peel off the cling film. Slice the parfait and serve with sticks of meringue. Any leftover parfait can go back in the freezer.

Indulge...

Serve the parfait smothered in hot chocolate sauce (see page 272).

Jam Doughnuts

I love jam doughnuts. I love, love, love jam doughnuts. I would almost go as far as to say I could live off jam doughnuts forever. They are one of the things that remind me of great Sunday fundays spent at markets in Melbourne, where a bag of these pillowy, sugar-coated balls of loveliness would cost just 50 cents.

As it now takes 24 hours to get to that market in Melbourne I simply make my own. Lots of them*.

Makes 24

1 x 7g sachet dried active yeast

50g caster sugar

30ml warm water

450g strong white flour

75g custard powder

10g salt

240ml milk

40g unsalted butter

2 eggs

3 litres vegetable oil, for deep- frying

For coating and filling

150g caster sugar

200g strawberry jam

You will need a stand mixer fitted with a K hook for this

Make the dough

In a cup, mix the yeast and a pinch of sugar with the warm water. Stir so the yeast and sugar dissolve.

Put the flour and custard powder into your stand mixer bowl with the salt and the remaining sugar.

Warm the milk and butter in a small pan over a low heat until the butter has melted. Turn off the heat. Crack your eggs into the warm butter and beat them in, then pour in the yeast mixture. You now have a batch of wet mixture and a batch of dry mixture.

Turn the mixer on. Quickly pour the wet mixture into the dry mixture. Now leave the machine on a medium speed to knead the dough for 10 minutes until it is smooth and stretchy – the dough should be really sticky.

Rest it

Take the hook out of the bowl, and cover the bowl with a clean tea towel. Leave it somewhere warm to prove for an hour, until doubled in size.

Slap the dough and it will deflate, like a balloon. Scrape the dough out of the bowl onto a lightly floured surface. Using a dough scraper or a butter knife, cut the dough into four and then divide each portion into six (it's easiest to work with it like this – you want 24 pieces in total). Roll each portion of dough into a ball and place on a floured tray, spaced apart. Cover the dough with oiled cling film and leave to rise again for about 45 minutes, until they've nearly doubled in size.

Patience, patience....

* By the way, stale, these make an awesome bread and butter pudding.

Jam Doughnuts

Cook the doughnuts

Take the cling film off the dough balls and using the palm of your hand, gently press down a little on each one so that it looks more like an ice hockey puck than a ball.

Pour the vegetable oil into a deep pan (or use a deep fat fryer) and heat the oil to 170°C. Put the sugar for coating the doughnuts on a plate.

Fry the doughnuts, six at a time, for 3–4 minutes each side, turning the doughnuts with a slotted spoon as they bob around the surface, until they are golden brown on each side. Lift the doughnuts out of the oil and immediately roll in the sugar to coat.

Fill them

Spoon the jam into a piping bag fitted with a little nozzle. Push the nozzle into the centre of each ball and pipe in as much jam as you can. Devour.

I love mine dipped in custard, just like this...

Or try...

Fill the doughnuts with thick custard (see page 270) or chocolate sauce (see page 272).

Coat the doughnuts in space dust or popping candy or let them cool and ice them.

Pistachio Baklava

It took me a long time to gather up the courage to venture into the Middle Eastern and Greek sweet shops that lined many Melbourne streets. Since then I've not looked back – sugar and spice and all things nice. Few people understand the beauty of baklava because it's so often dry and too sweet. This magic filo pastry dessert should be sweet and sticky but not sickly.

Makes about 24 pieces

125g caster sugar

120ml water

juice of ½ lemon

300g blanched almonds

300g pistachios

2 teaspoons ground cinnamon

60g dark chocolate chips

125g unsalted butter

12 sheets filo pastry

1 teaspoon orange blossom water (be careful – different brands, different strengths)

Heat the oven to 180°C/gas 4.

Make the syrup

Put the sugar, water and lemon juice in a small pan and gently heat until the sugar dissolves, then bring to a rolling boil and cook for 5 minutes, stirring all the time, until the mixture has thickened to the consistency of maple syrup but not honey. If the syrup has thickened too much, just add a little water. Leave to cool.

Make the filling

Put the almonds in a separate small pan and toast over a medium heat, moving them around the pan, until they're golden and smelling of toasted nuts. When the almonds are toasted, drop in the pistachios and cook for 2 minutes to toast them a little too. Transfer all the nuts to a food processor and pulse (do not blend!) until the nuts are the texture of pearl barley.

Put the nuts, half the syrup and the cinnamon and chocolate chips into a large bowl and stir everything together so that it is all mixed up and sticky. Melt the butter in a small pan and keep warm.

And then...

Pistachio Baklava

Layer up

Butter a 38 x 25 x 2.5cm baking tray with a little of the melted butter. Place one sheet of the filo in the base of the tray and trim it to fit. Remove it from the tray and use it as a template to trim all the sheets of filo pastry to this size.

Now it's assembly time. Put the first layer of filo in the baking tray and brush with a little butter. Repeat until you have six layers on the base of the tray. Spread the nut mixture evenly over the top. Cover with the remaining sheets of filo, brushing each layer with butter and pour any remaining butter over the top layer of pastry.

With a sharp knife, cut the baklava into elongated diamonds. Bake in the oven for 20 minutes or until the top is lightly golden and crispy.

Almost there...

Meanwhile, mix together the remaining syrup and orange blossom water and set to one side.

When the baklava is cooked, brush the top with the orange syrup so it soaks in and is all glossy and sticky and sweet – you may have a little syrup left over. Leave to cool, uncovered, for a little before eating the whole lot!

Panna Cotta with Stewed Rhubarb

My favourite creamy dessert is panna cotta, an Italian 'cooked cream' that I can only describe as milky and bosom-like (in the best Pre-Raphaelite tradition), with a few vanilla-seed freckles.

I like my rhubarb to be firm and not boiled to death so I bake it with sugar and vanilla to release its delicious juices. The result: a firm, syrupy, sticky fruit rather than a watery pulp. Yum. This stewed rhubarb is also delicious served with some clotted cream or ice cream, or anything actually.

Serves 4

For the panna cotta

600ml double cream

200ml whole milk

100g caster sugar

1 vanilla pod, split lengthways and seeds scraped out

3 gelatine leaves

For the stewed rhubarb

400g rhubarb, trimmed and chopped (you can chop the rhubarb into any size you like; I like mine as long as a pencil)

100g caster sugar

1 vanilla pod, split lengthways

You will need four 150ml pudding moulds

Make the panna cotta

Put the cream, milk, sugar and vanilla pod and seeds in a pan. Bring to the boil, then immediately take it off the heat and leave to cool a little – about 5 minutes. Soak the gelatine in cold water.

Lift the vanilla pod out of the cream (wash it, dry it and put it in your sugar jar to make vanilla sugar). Squeeze out the excess water from the gelatine, then drop it into the infused cream and stir until the gelatine has dissolved. Continue to stir to cool the mixture.

Pour the cream into four 150ml pudding moulds and leave to set in the fridge overnight. And that's it – making panna cotta is easy.

The next day, stew the rhubarb

Heat the oven to 140°C/gas 1.

Spread out the rhubarb in a roasting tin, pour over the sugar and place the vanilla pod on top. Cover the tin with kitchen foil, sealing it tightly, and bake in the oven for 40 minutes.

Serve

Dip a knife into boiling water and run it around the edges of the moulds to loosen the panna cotta. Turn each one out onto a plate. Spoon the rhubarb alongside.

Variations

Stewed plums or peaches.

Set the panna cotta in small bowls and top with sauces or jelly.

Pistachio and Cardamom Cake

I find the scent of cardamom romantic and evocative and the aroma as it cooks always makes me feel like I am making something really special and generous. This cake is just that: generous, soft, soggy, sweet and heady with spice. It tastes good when it has been allowed to cool but when eaten hot it is a beauty and may even involve you in a promise.

Makes 1 cake

115g self-raising flour

1 teaspoon baking powder

115g golden caster sugar

2 teaspoons cardamom powder

1 teaspoon ground cinnamon

115g butter, plus extra for greasing

2 eggs

1 teaspoon rose water

1 teaspoon vanilla extract

150ml soured cream

75g pistachio nuts, chopped

25g walnuts, chopped

For the whipped cream

70g double cream

3 teaspoons vanilla extract

1 teaspoon orange blossom water (be careful – different brands, different strengths)

3 teaspoons caster sugar

Heat the oven to 170°C/gas 4. Grease a 23cm cake tin.

Sift the flour, baking powder and half the sugar into a large bowl. Add the cardamom and cinnamon and mix well.

Use an electric whisk to beat the butter with the remaining sugar until white, break an egg into the mixture and beat well, then do the same with the other egg. Fold in the flour mixture and then add the rose water, vanilla extract, soured cream and chopped nuts and beat until fluffy.

Pour the mixture into the tin. Cover with kitchen foil and bake for 25 minutes. Take the foil off and bake for a further 5 minutes or until a skewer inserted into the centre of the cake comes out clean. Take it out of the oven, leave it in the tin for 5 minutes to cool a little, then turn it out onto a wire rack to cool.

The cream

Put the cream, vanilla extract, orange blossom water and caster sugar in a small bowl and whip it until thick and peaky. Serve the cake with big dollops of cream.

Go posh...

Scatter with rose petals and chopped nuts to serve.

Drizzle the cream with lavender honey.

Peach Upside-down Cake

My nanna used to grow lots of fruit in her back garden – ladyfinger bananas, passion fruit, apples, limes, lemons, mulberries and strawberries – but my favourite were the peaches. Whenever I cook this cake I feel as though I could be 9 years old again, standing next to Nanna on a sunny Saturday, peaches just picked from the tree at the side of the house and the smell of her perfume and the wood-burning stove.

Makes 1 cake

5–6 peaches, cut in half and stones removed

400g caster sugar

1 vanilla pod, split in half lengthways and seeds scraped out

200g plain flour

1½ teaspoons baking powder

200g butter

4 eggs

30ml milk

icing sugar, for dusting

Heat the oven to 180°C/gas 4. Line the base of a 23cm springform cake tin with baking parchment.

Prep the peaches

Pop the peaches in a large pan with 200g of the sugar and the vanilla seeds and pod, cover with water – just enough to cover the fruit – and bring to the boil. Turn off the heat and cover with a lid and leave them for 20 minutes.

Make the cake batter

Sift the flour and the baking powder together into a bowl three times to aerate.

Beat the butter and the remaining sugar until white and doubled in size (an electric whisk is good for this). Add the eggs one at a time, beating until well mixed, then add the sifted flour and milk and mix well.

Lift the peaches out of their cooking liquid and arrange the wet peaches, cut-side down, over the base of the cake tin. Pour the cake batter over the peaches and bake in the oven for 25–30 minutes or until a skewer inserted into the centre of the cake comes out clean. Allow the cake to cool in the tin a little – about 10–15 minutes – then gently turn out onto a plate and carefully peel off the paper.

Leave to sit for 30 minutes. Dust with icing sugar and serve warm.

Swap in...

Pears, apricots, cherries or apples with cinnamon all work well instead of peaches.

Index

Entries in bold indicate a photograph.

First published in 2015

by HEADLINE PUBLISHING GROUP

2

Cataloguing in Publication Data is available from the British Library

Hardback ISBN 9781472225856

Designed by Mark Harper at Bonbon London

Photography: Yuki Sugiura

Food styling: Lizzie Kamenetzky

Food styling assistant: Poppy Mahon, and thanks also to Emma Miller

Prop styling: Cynthia Inions

Recipe editor: Imogen Fortes

Repro at BORN Group

Printed and bound in Germany by Mohn Media

HEADLINE PUBLISHING GROUP

An Hachette UK Company

Carmelite House

50 Victoria Embankment

London EC4 0DZ

www.headline.co.uk

www.hachette.co.uk

Acknowledgements

Over the past 12 months I have had a ball writing and cooking for this book, but of course, no man is an island and the only way a book like this comes together is because a caring team of wonderful people gets stuck in and makes it happen.

My thanks are in no particular order… (Maybe in order of appearance?)

Jo Carlton, thank you for continuing to believe in me, for pushing the boundaries and listening to me when I rant. I know it's not often but I do rant.

Jonathan Conway, for putting 'the deal' together: you are very clever and a really nice bloke. Thanks.

My Lisa, for pushing me, making me stick to my guns and listening when I needed you to listen. You rock my world.

'The team', as I have now collectively decided to call you, you all know who you are. A great big sloppy Aussie kiss. Thank you.

Yuki Sugiura, you are one heck of a photographer. You are so lovely, your pictures are beautiful and you let me be the cook. The greatest respect. Thank you! And to the wonderful Clarence for all the teas and laughter – we really missed you on our last day.

Cynthia Inions, a stylist who is indispensible. Thank you for working so hard and making the ordinary extraordinary, for taking my few thangs and making it my book. You are brill. See you soon.

Thanks to Mark Harper, a great chum and a man of calm and persistence. You slapped my smile all over this beautiful book and it looks and feels just the way I wanted it to.

Pictures of food don't just appear and I have to give a big hug and thanks to Lizzie Kamenetzky and Poppy Mahon, for working in my little kitchen and taking my food and ideas to the place they belong, on the pages of this book for all to be inspired by. I couldn't have done it without you.

If I could spell and write I would still ask for Imogen Fortes to edit my future books. Thank you for your patience, your attention to detail and for allowing me to use my words. What a joy.

Every team needs a captain and my captain is Muna Reyal. I bow to you. Your belief and trust has made this all possible.

And thank you to the rest of the Headline team, particularly Elizabeth Masters and Viviane Basset for getting *My Kind of Food* out there and spreading the word.

That's it until next time. Thank you for taking the time to read my book.